RIDE RIGHT WITH DANIEL STEWART

RIDE RIGHT WITH DANIEL STEWART

Balance Your Frame and Frame of Mind
with an Unmounted Workout and
Sport Psychology System

Daniel Stewart

Photographs by Ken Stewart and Joseph Huckestein
Illustrations by Maria Dickerson

Trafalgar Square Publishing
North Pomfret, Vermont

First published in 2004 by
Trafalgar Square Publishing
North Pomfret, Vermont 05053

Printed in China

The author has made every effort to obtain releases from all persons appearing in the photographs used in this book and all photographers. In some cases, however, the persons and photographers identities and whereabouts were unknown. Should any names become available, they will be credited in future editions, assuming permission is granted.

Disclaimer of Liability
The author and publisher shall have neither liability nor responsibility to any person or entity with respect to any loss or damage caused or alleged to be caused directly or indirectly by the information contained in this book. While the book is as accurate as the author can make it, there may be errors, omissions, and inaccuracies.

Library of Congress Cataloging-in-Publication Data

Stewart, Daniel.
Ride right with Daniel Stewart : balance your frame and frame of mind with an unmounted workout and sports psychology system / Daniel Stewart.
        p. cm.
ISBN 1-57076-281-3 (pbk.)
1. Horsemanship.   I. Title.
SF309.S835 2004
798.2—dc22

2004000006

Book design by Lynne Walker Design Studio
Typeface: Futura and Sabon

Color separations by Tenon & Polert Colour Scanning Ltd., Hong Kong

10 9 8 7 6 5 4 3 2 1

DEDICATION

For my wife, Severine, and my son, Luca.

TABLE OF CONTENTS

ACKNOWLEDGMENTS

Perhaps the greatest pleasure I've had from writing this book has been the opportunity of working with so many incredibly talented and horse-passionate people. I'd like to express my sincere thanks to Stephanie Beauchamp, Maria Dickerson, Elisabeth McMillan, Mary Jo Lord, Christopher Maga, Annika Washburn, Erin Barrett, Barbara Grassmyer, and Hannah Childs for allowing me to mold their normally great riding postures into imperfect shapes for the sake of the photographs. As a result of all your efforts readers will be able to see and understand how imperfect riders can create imperfect horses.

I am also grateful to Joseph Huckestein and Ken Stewart for the time and effort they put into taking the photographs and to Maria Dickerson for her illustrations.

I'd also like to extend a very special thanks to all of the instructors in my life who dedicated their time and passion to develop my skills as a horseman and teacher. There are, however, three remarkable coaches and riders to whom I am especially indebted. Mary Lutz and Art Priesz Jr. from the United States Equestrian Team (USET), and Denise Avolio from the National Disabled Sports Association (NDSA) had the courage and conviction to take a chance on asking a relatively unknown riding instructor to become part of their coaching staff. Day in and day out they dedicate an inhuman amount of time and effort to their teams, and bringing me on board as their sport psychology and biomechanic specialist was just additional proof that they're willing to do anything to help their riders succeed. The next pitcher of margaritas is on me!

I am also deeply indebted to Trafalgar Square Publishing, especially the publisher and my editor Caroline Robbins, and the managing editor, Martha Cook. Where the two of you found the strength and patience to turn an old riding instructor into a new author, I'll never know. Your unwavering attitude and generous assistance not only helped me to complete this book, it also taught me how to take more pride in every new task I undertake in life. Thank you again for your helpful suggestions, indispensable criticisms, and confidence.

For my wife Severine I thank you for all your patience and support. I admit it wasn't easy living with a computer-illiterate rider who had to spend eight hours a day writing a book, but you handled it with poise and understanding. To my son Luca, thank you for coming along just in time to provide me with the motivation that I needed to complete something so important to me.

My final thanks goes to every single big-hearted horse I've had the privilege of riding. I thank you for the lessons you taught, the discipline you instilled, the understanding you shared, and the patience you bestowed upon me. Through your unspoken ways you became my best friend and the best teacher I could have ever hoped for. I never have, and never will stop marveling at your ability to maintain such a positive attitude and graceful conformation—especially when asked to work with so many riders who are so positively ungraceful!

INTRODUCTION

The horse and rider relationship is truly a special one, and it should not be taken for granted. Many riders "blame" their horses for being stiff going in one direction, for preferring one lead over another, or being heavy on the forehand, but what they don't realize—or won't admit—is that it is they who are stiff on one side or feel more comfortable cantering on one lead rather than the other. Riders don't do this on purpose. When they blame their horse for a problem they have created by their riding, they are usually simply unaware of their physical flaws and their effects.

I cannot count the number of times I have told students that they are collapsing their torsos to one side, placing more weight in one stirrup, and sitting on one seat bone, only to receive an uncomprehending stare in return! They have no idea they are riding this way. I now realize that riders have difficulty sensing their poor balance and asymmetry. And, if they cannot "feel" the problem, they cannot correct themselves.

I recently met a woman who on discovering that I videotaped riders and analysed their position, jumped at this opportunity. She told me that her horse was extremely stiff on the right, and that none of her experts—farrier, veterinarian, horse chiropractor and acupuncturist, and magnet technician—was able to locate his problem. After a few seconds of watching her ride, it was obvious why. The problem was her. She shifted her hips three inches to the right, collapsed the entire left side of her body, pinched with her right knee, and placed more weight in her right seat bone and stirrup. She had spent an enormous amount of money to discover her horse's "problem," when all she had needed to do was look at herself.

A rider should be an athlete in the truest sense, yet many riders fail to see themselves as such. They have no qualms about spending hundreds of hours, and sometime thousands of dollars each year making their horses a little better, but don't spend any time or money improving themselves.

Some just forget—they warm up their horses but not their own bodies—while others simply lack basic knowledge of human anatomy. I was reminded of this recently: a good friend who possesses possibly the greatest knowledge of equine physiology of any rider I know—he probably knows a dozen places to take his horse's pulse—wasn't able to complete one of my simple stamina tests because he couldn't find his own pulse!

In order for my riding students to become more aware of their riding position, several years ago, I developed an unmounted exercise program for them to do at home. At first, this homework consisted of a few balance and posture exercises performed while standing on an unstable surface like a balance board. It didn't take long before I noticed their riding performance improve, which they attributed to a heightened sense of their own body awareness and a better ability to remain mentally focused in the saddle. These exercises were having a positive effect on their *frame* and, as a bonus, their *frame of mind*, too.

Since then, I have further developed those basic exercises, and the result is the program that I present in this book. When you develop a good *frame* and *frame of mind,* you will be confident that your flaws aren't interfering with your horse's performance, and you can concentrate on making him more comfortable and happy by correctly interpreting and correcting his stiffness and performance difficulties. It is this kind of awareness and respect that separates good riders from great ones.

☀

PART ONE

FRAME AND FORM

ALL RIDERS HAVE UNIQUE AND SPECIAL BODY SHAPES and like our horses, no two of us are built exactly alike. We come in a variety of shapes and sizes ranging from tall to short, big to little, and fat to skinny. All body types have the capacity of achieving riding success. While one body type may seem better suited to a specific riding discipline, there's simply no reason you can't succeed at any riding goal you set your mind (and body) to. Your body, regardless of shape, weight, or size, should never be considered a handicap, but, instead, a tool that can be finely tuned to help you ride your best. I've worked with hundreds of heavy riders who've learn to ride in a light manner (and just as many lightweight riders who ride in a heavy manner), and I think I speak for all horses when I say they care more about how you carry your weight than how much weight you actually carry. Learn to take pride in your body's uniqueness, do everything you can to improve upon what you already have, and use your frame to your best advantage.

> *You know it's impossible to achieve great riding success with a horse that's stiff, crooked, weak, and unbalanced, but have you ever stopped to think that a horse has just as difficult a time achieving great success with a rider who's stiff, crooked, weak, and unbalanced?*

CHAPTER ONE

HUMAN BODY SHAPES

To help you understand how your body affects your ability to *Ride Right,* I've developed a classification system that divides body shapes into seven different categories. Once you have a better understanding of how your shape and size influences your riding, you can develop an unmounted program to solve your mounted imperfections. Before starting you must keep three things in mind:

1. Even though your body shape is determined genetically, it can be altered by changes in behavioral patterns. For instance, if you are naturally slender, you can still become overweight if you ignore good eating and fitness habits. Likewise, if you are overweight, you can still become slim and fit through proper diet and exercise.

2. You likely have characteristics of more than one category.

3. Each body shape is labeled after a familiar breed of horse to make the category easier to understand.

Immediately following each body-shape discussion is a brief section called *framework* where I introduce the kind of unmounted "work" that will best improve your *frame.*

Categories

Shetland
You have a *Shetland* body shape if you're small, lightweight, and have short limbs. You gain weight evenly but aren't prone to becoming overweight. Because you have short legs, you may find it a challenge to apply leg aids. On the positive side, you have a low center of gravity and, therefore, a good natural sense of balance. You also have small muscles which, as long as they're fit, are to your advantage because the larger your muscles are, the greater the chance of them becoming stiff and inflexible.

Shetland Framework
Increase your strength and stamina, but in order to avoid the danger of decreasing your flexibility, only perform *lightweight* strength exercises, and participate in a stretching program. Remember that improved strength and stamina will only make your riding better, as long as it doesn't interfere with your suppleness.

Connemara
You have a *Connemara* body shape if you're

Give your body a tune-up!

When a car is no longer in good shape, it's called a lemon. When your body's no longer in good shape, it starts to look like a lemon. Below is a list of things an auto mechanic might say about your car, and what it means for your body.

Car	Body
Your belts need to be checked	When was the last time you saw your belt?
The tires need to be balanced	One side of your body is stronger and stiffer
The radiator is leaking	You're out of shape and sweat like a horse
The carburetor uses too much air	You get out of breath easily
The battery needs to be replaced	You have no energy and need to get fit
Nice spare tire	Nice spare tire!

short or medium in height, and wide around the middle. You have short limbs, little muscular definition, and gain weight easily. Unfortunately, as you gain weight, the girths of your body and legs increase, making it difficult for you to maintain a deep seat and good leg contact with your horse. On the positive side, your short body has a relatively low center of gravity and, therefore, a good natural sense of balance. This is a blessing because your legs may not have sufficient length or contact to overcome a serious loss of equilibrium in the saddle.

Connemara Framework

While it's possible to be overweight and ride well, your horse will appreciate it if you slim down. The best way to accomplish this is by working on the stamina exercises and practicing the healthy eating habits outlined in this book (see p. 131).

Quarter Horse

You have a *Quarter Horse* body shape if you're medium in height and muscular. You have a narrow waist, broad shoulders and chest, flat stomach, and muscular limbs. While strength is important and often associated with athletic performance, too much can hinder your ability to *Ride Right* because strength decreases your flexibility and supple-

ness. Due to your large upper body, your center of gravity is high, a conformation that usually causes poor balance.

Quarter Horse Framework

Improve your overall flexibility and balance. Avoid developing stiff muscles by performing the *lightweight* strength and stamina exercises in this book and follow each session with a good stretching program (see p. 107).

Thoroughbred

You have a *Thoroughbred* body shape if your height is medium or tall, you have long, slender limbs, and small well-defined muscles. You don't gain weight easily, but when you do, it usually ends up in your midsection as a "spare tire." Since your body is long and your hips are narrow, you have a high center of gravity and a narrow base of support—both of which can cause balance and symmetry problems. Thankfully, your legs are long so they can help you out whenever you feel less than 100 percent stable in the saddle.

Thoroughbred Framework

Improve your balance and symmetry. Coordination-enhancing exercises will help you use your long body and limbs in the most effective way possible (see p. 153).

Warmblood

You have a *Warmblood* body shape if you're tall and shapely. Women have an "hourglass" figure, and men are well sculpted, without being overly muscular. This type of athletic build should help you attain success in any riding discipline, though your center of gravity is high and you may be challenged by riding situations that require a lot of balance.

Warmblood Framework

While your long legs and athletic ability help you overcome periodic lapses in equilibrium, you can learn to *Ride Right* by improving your balance and symmetry.

Anglo-Arabian

You have an *Anglo-Arabian* body shape if you have a thin, lightweight upper body, wide hips, and robust thighs. The term "pear-shaped" is often used. You have a low center of gravity and a wide base of support, which are the two most important ingredients of good balance. Be careful not to gain too much weight in your hip and thigh area. This decreases the mobility and suppleness of your lower torso, and sacrifices the contact between your legs and your horse.

Anglo-Arabian Framework

Participate in a stretching program that targets your hips and a stamina program that targets your thighs. Avoid letting your hips become too large by paying close attention to good eating habits (see p. 131).

Draft Horse

You have a *Draft Horse* body shape if you're tall and have big bones, a broad chest and shoulders, thick midsection, flat behind, and solid limbs. Since much of your weight is carried in your upper body, your center of gravity is quite high. Your body mass (which can either be muscular or fat) is so great that it often interferes with your flexibility and ability to ride in a graceful manner. Unfortunately, even if you suffer a small loss of balance, your size exaggerates the situation thus creating an even greater problem.

Draft Horse Framework

Increase your balance, symmetry, stamina, and flexibility, while decreasing your body mass with the help of the stamina exercises and healthy eating tips (see p. 131).

The Difference Between the Male and Female Frame

In order to understand how the many differences between male and female riders affect your ability to *Ride Right*, you need to look much deeper than just muscles and mascara.

On average, men weigh 25 to 30 pounds more, and are 3 to 4 inches taller than women. A woman's body is more flexible because her joints and ligaments are suppler, and she has less muscle mass to interfere with her body's range of motion. Another difference—one that has a very influential effect on riding performance—is the hip area. A woman has a broad pelvis area created by outward-facing hip sockets and widely spaced seat bones that angle outward, while a man has a narrow pelvis area formed by forward-facing hip

> ## The two pieces of the balance puzzle
>
> *"Base of support" is the distance between two or more weight-bearing points on an object, and "center of gravity" is the exact center of a body's mass. The wider your base of support (hips), and the lower your center of gravity, the more balanced you'll be.*

sockets and almost vertical seat bones (figs. 1.1 A–D). The female's base of support (the distance between her two weight-bearing seat bones) is wider than the male's, and thus gives her an advantage when it comes to balance and consequent security in the saddle (fig. 1.2).

In a woman's pelvis, the tailbone isn't under her spine like the male's tailbone, but instead sticks well out and away from her lumbar region. Consequently, female riders tend to have hollow lower backs and need to constantly roll their tailbones under and forward (by contracting their stomach muscles) to create a flat, low back while in the saddle. Since the male's tailbone is more naturally tucked under his spine, he doesn't need to expend as much effort to flatten his back.

Two other riding issues related to the pelvis are *knock-knees* and *bowlegs* (fig. 1.3). *Knock-knee,* a condition affecting many female riders, is caused by the wide width of the female pelvis area and its outward-facing hip sockets. Characterized by an inward inclination of the legs from the hips to the knees, this misalignment causes the female rider to

1.1 A–D Pelvic Structure

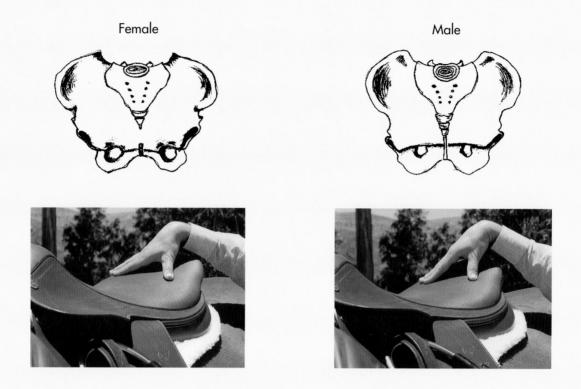

Female

Male

Drawings A and B and photos C and D illustrate the female and male pelvic structure, respectively. The hand in the photos shows the width difference, and as you can see in C, the female pelvis is wider, thus providing a wider base of support.

1.2 A & B Hip Socket and Tailbone

Female

Male

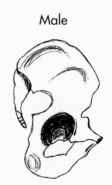

These diagrams show the difference between the female and male hip socket and tailbone.

"pinch" with her knees while standing, walking, and riding. Difficulty achieving a relaxed leg position, a lower leg that swings, trouble applying leg aids, stiffness in the hips and lower back, and knee pain are some of the riding problems associated with this conformation. The *bowleg* condition, a misalignment similar to knock-knees because it's characterized by an inclination (albeit outward) of the thigh from the hip to the knee, is usually caused by the narrow pelvis, vertical hip bones, and front-facing hip sockets of the male pelvic area. Unlike knock-knees, this condition can be advantageous because it allows you to wrap your legs more effectively and naturally around the barrel-shaped body of your horse. Good leg contact, effective leg aids, and a deep seat are some of the advantages related to this kind of rider conformation.

In general, a woman is somewhat triangle-shaped because she has narrow shoulders and wide hips, while a man is like an upside-down triangle with wide shoulders, back, and chest, and narrow hips (figs. 1.4 A & B). The female conformation is more suited to balance because the upside-down shape of the male triangle is less stable than a triangle sitting on its wide base of support. In addition, most of a woman's weight is located in her hip area, while much of a man's weight is located in his upper torso. As a result, the woman's center of gravity is usually lower than the man's. When

1.3 Knock-Knees and Bowlegs

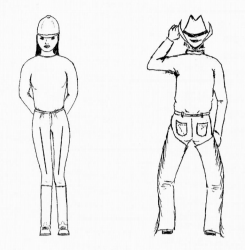

Notice how the knock-kneed condition causes an inward inclination of the rider's thigh, while bowlegged causes an outward inclination.

you take into consideration that the male rider's center of gravity is already three or four inches higher due to his taller height, it's obvious that the female rider's center of gravity is located much closer to the ground. Add the woman's wide base of support to her low center of gravity, and she has a real advantage when it comes to balance in the saddle.

I once taught a rider who referred to men as

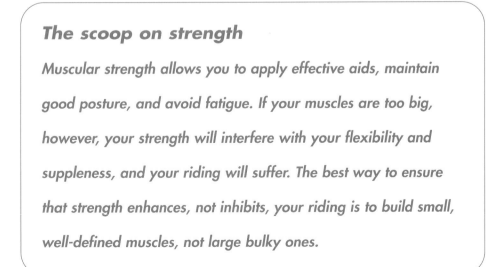

The scoop on strength

Muscular strength allows you to apply effective aids, maintain good posture, and avoid fatigue. If your muscles are too big, however, your strength will interfere with your flexibility and suppleness, and your riding will suffer. The best way to ensure that strength enhances, not inhibits, your riding is to build small, well-defined muscles, not large bulky ones.

the "stronger sex." While she may have simply been using the expression to point out the difference in strength between men and women, it was in no way meant as a compliment to male riders. As I mentioned earlier, while the male body is usually more muscular than the female, the location and size of the man's muscles often cause more problems than they solve. Carrying muscular weight in the chest, shoulders, and arms usually results in stiff shoulder and arm joints, poor upper body flexibility, and less than perfect dexterity. It's also not uncommon for male riders to believe that they can control their horses with strength alone, an attitude that can cause them to ride in a mechanical manner. On the other hand, the majority of strength in the female body is in her legs and hips, and this allows her upper body to remain supple and light while her lower body is permitted to move in a controlled manner.

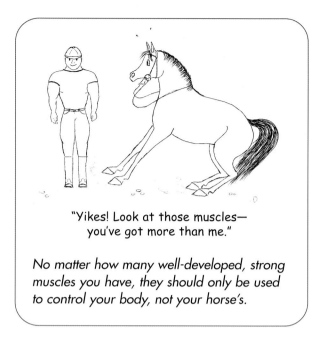

"Yikes! Look at those muscles—you've got more than me."

No matter how many well-developed, strong muscles you have, they should only be used to control your body, not your horse's.

Last, but not least, a woman's bones are lighter and more porous than a man's, and while a rider with lightweight bones may be a horse's best friend, they're more susceptible to injury and provide less protection from the shock and micro-vibrations that travel through the rider's body.

Female Framework

- Most of your strength is located in your leg and hip area, so try to achieve a better body balance by improving the strength and stamina of your back, abdominal muscles, shoulders, and arms.

- There's no such thing as *too much* balance, so participate in balance-enhancing exercises whenever you can.

- Your body has one dominant side so do exercises that bring the left and right side of your body into perfect symmetry.

- If you suffer from knock-knees, alleviate some of your discomfort and mounted problems by strengthening the muscles, tendons, and ligaments on the outside of your knees, thighs, and hips, and stretching those on the inside.

1.4 A & B Triangle of Balance

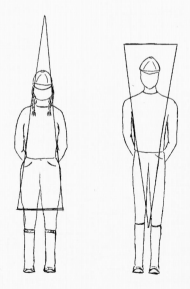

Narrow shoulders combined with wide hips create a regular triangle with the base at the bottom. Wide shoulders and narrow hips make an upside-down triangle. Which triangle is more stable? When it comes to balance, it's clear that the female has an advantage.

- Your bones are porous and the only way to increase their density (without taking medication) is by performing *lightweight* strength-training exercises. The mild stress your muscles place on your bones is responsible for this change.

Male Framework

- You likely have a high center of gravity and narrow base of support, so participate in exercises that enhance your balance.

- Your joints, tendons, ligaments, and muscles are stiff so increase your flexibility by warming up, stretching, and cooling-down when exercising or riding.

- Your body has one dominant side so do exercises that bring the left and right side of your body into perfect symmetry.

- Strong chest muscles lead to a rounded upper back so teach your body to open its shoulders naturally by strengthening your back and stretching your chest.

- Large muscles (especially those of the upper body) lessen your balance and increase stiffness so avoid developing them by only doing a *lightweight* strength-training or stamina program.

Your Horse's Frame

Equine experts use a classification system to define a horse's frame. According to their 9-point system, a 1 indicates an extremely malnourished horse, a 5 or 6 indicates a healthy horse, and a 9 indicates a severely obese one. Their classification focuses on six different aspects of the equine frame including the amount of fat on the neck, withers, tail head, ribs, shoulders, and running down the horse's back.

A healthy horse is defined as one that has a flat back; ribs that can be felt but are not visible; smoothly rounded withers; little or no crease down the back; shoulders and neck that blend smoothly into the body; and a back that blends smoothly with the hindquarters at the tail.

Conclusion

In this section, I've introduced you to a variety of different categories that distinguish your body from other riders. These categories should help you to better understand and appreciate the way in which your body affects your ability to *Ride Right*. As you may have noticed, every body type is associated with a few negative and positive aspects. There really isn't a rider body shape that is truly perfect. While some shapes may seem more desirable than others, you have the ability to build upon what you already have, and self-

A horse doesn't care if his rider is a little overweight for her height, as long as she rides "light." To him, it's more important how she carries her weight, rather than how much weight she carries!

improvement always leads to greater horse and rider success. While you may never be able to attain the perfect body, it's really the journey toward that end that's most important. It shows an incredible dedication to your sport when you're willing to help your horse by improving upon your own natural imperfections. In this book, you'll learn several physical and mental skills that can help you accomplish this goal.

*

PART TWO
FRAME AND FUNCTION

RIDER BIOMECHANICS IS A TERM USED TO DESCRIBE the way in which your body functions and interacts with the body of your horse. Any time you suffer a "biomechanic imperfection," your horse mirrors the fault. For instance, it's impossible for a horse to be perfectly balanced or symmetrical if you're not. And, one imperfection always leads to another. You can't ride in a supple and relaxed manner, for example, if you constantly hold your breath. It's interesting to note that these imperfections work in reverse as well, that is, it's impossible to breathe well if you constantly ride in a tense and stiff manner.

CHAPTER TWO

SYMMETRY

In Part One, I introduced you to seven different rider shapes and discussed the affect each one has on performance. Starting with this chapter, I'll discuss how to improve your *frame* (and, in doing so, the *frame* of your horse) by resolving some of your body's natural imperfections. (Later, I will outline how to improve your *frame of mind* by resolving mental issues such as fear, anxiety, and doubt.) *Symmetry, balance, breathing, body awareness, strength, stamina,* and *flexibility* are these attributes, and while each one is essential, it's the mastery of all seven that'll ultimately allow you to *Ride Right.*

You're said to be *symmetrical* if you possess an equal amount of strength, stamina, balance, flexibility, and coordination on both sides of your body. You're able to place an equal amount of weight in each foot and seat bone, impart effective leg and rein aids with both arms and legs, and help your horse overcome problems on either side of his body. Even though you may feel symmetrical, there's a possibility that you may be suffering from one kind of asymmetry or another. Riding better in one direction, feeling more comfortable on one lead, and always looking to one side are three indications of asymmetry. This is a very common riding problem because it can be caused by so many different factors (figs. 2.1 to 2.3).

2.1 A–C Symmetry

Good symmetry: the centerline of Stephanie's body (see black tape) is in line with her horse's centerline, and she has identical weight in both stirrups.

"C" asymmetry: Stephanie's body is in a "C" shape. Her hips are shifted to the left with more weight put in that stirrup, and her torso, shoulders, and head have "collapsed" to the right.

"S" asymmetry: her body is in an "S" shape. Her torso has collapsed to the left, and her head is dropped to the right.

2.2 A–C Jumping Asymmetry

In A and B, the rider is ducking to one side (note the uneven stirrups in B), and in C, where the rider is too far forward and displaying "chicken elbows" by way of compensation, you can see the unlevel saddle caused by her crookedness and too much weight in her right leg.

2.3 Riding Asymmetry

The act of neck reining using just one arm can cause asymmetry: note this Western rider's right buttock and leg are dropped as she prepares to turn right.

Causes of Asymmetry in Riders

1. You (like your horse) are born with one dominant side. (Very rarely is a baby born ambidextrous, that is, with the ability to use left and right sides equally.) This physical imbalance leads to the labels "right" and "left-handed." As a result of this imbalance, you use your dominant side to perform the majority of your daily riding skills, such as picking a hoof, carrying your saddle, cinching a girth, and pulling a mane (figs. 2.4 A–C). While it's common and understandable to use your dominant side to complete your daily chores, doing so only serves to accentuate the imbalance. When you combine your genetic asymmetry with the tendency to overuse your dominant side, it's a foregone conclusion that one side of your body will become stronger and more coordinated than the other.

2. Muscular strength is directly related to flexibility—the stronger the muscle, the less supple it'll be. Unfortunately, if the muscles on one side of your body become stronger than the muscles on the other, a strength and suppleness imbalance can occur in the muscles and joints (hinges) of your body, including your hips, shoulders, elbows, wrists, ankles, and knees. This kind of inequality can have a major effect on your riding because it makes it difficult for you to remain balanced in the center of your saddle and hinders the ability to impart equally effective leg and rein aids.

3. Behavioral patterns (jobs, recreational activities, favorite sports) also play a major role in determining symmetry. A receptionist who constantly cradles a phone on her left shoulder so that she can write with her right hand is a good example of someone who lets her job affect her symmetry. Many sports, especially those that require the use of a ball (tennis, for example) also accentuate genetic asymmetry because you only use your dominant hand to hit the ball. Behavioral patterns are not limited to physical activities: a student of mine constantly rode with her hips and saddle shifted to the left because she always car-ried her baby in her left arm and nothing at all in her right. Since so much weight was being carried on her left side, she unconsciously shifted her hips to the left to support some of the weight. When I asked her why she didn't even-out the load, she said that she kept her right hand free to open doors, pay the taxi, and feed her baby a bottle. This rider is a good example of someone who lets her behavioral patterns affect her symmetry, and therefore, her riding as well.

4. Athletic injuries of the type caused by non-contact sports also accentuate your body's imbalance. When an injury occurs, it usually does so on the dominant side of your body. *Tennis elbow* is a good example because it normally only affects the right elbow of right-handed players. The real problem is not so much *where* on the body the injury occurs, but the *physical response* your body employs to protect and heal it. This process, called *guarding*, protects the injured area by increasing muscular stiffness, and therefore stability, around it. If you've broken a bone or suffered a serious injury in the past, you may find that the body part is still stiff, even if the injury occurred many years ago. This mechanism,

2.4 A–C Asymmetry

Everyday activities with your horse can encourage you to develop an unbalanced posture.

A different kind of hip angle

Normally, the phrase "hip angle" refers to the angle created between the front of your thighs and your stomach—the term is used when describing the posting trot as opening and closing your hip angle (referring to the change that this angle undergoes when your hips post forward and backward).

However, I use the term *hip angle* to describe another very important aspect of hip conformation. If your hips shift to one side while riding (thus placing more weight in one seat bone and stirrup), the angles created between the side of your torso and outside of your thighs are unequal—one is a sharper angle while the other a softer, more rounded angle. When your hips are symmetrical, so too are these new hip angles.

2.5 Hip Angle

Note that the angle created between Maria's left thigh and the left side of her torso is narrower than the angle made by her right side. To be able to ride in symmetry, these angles need to be identical.

which initially sets out to help you, actually hurts you later by increasing the imbalance between your left and right sides.

5. Physical fitness plays a role in symmetry. When your body is physically fatigued, you shift your hips to one side and place more weight on that foot. I call this position your *discomfort zone* because even though it feels comfortable, it teaches you to do the same thing when you get tired in the saddle, something that will eventually cause your horse discomfort.

6. Physical genetic defects, such as *scoliosis* (characterized by a left-to-right misalignment of the spine), also create asymmetrical problems. These conditions make it virtually impossible to obtain a relaxed, balanced, and symmetrical posture. Unlike the other causes of asymmetry, genetic defects are difficult and time-consuming to correct, and even with the assistance of doctor or chiropractor may never completely disappear.

Rider Asymmetry— Effects on the Horse

Poor rider symmetry, while certainly affecting both horse and rider, is not caused (but may be exaggerated) by the interaction between the horse and rider. It's caused by one or more of the six factors I just outlined, so trying to solve poor symmetry by just improving your horse will simply not do the trick. The only way you'll be able to achieve a truly symmetrical body is to become aware of the situations that cause your asymmetry, and then change them. In Chapter Six, page 153, I introduce you to a series of exercises that can help you achieve this.

You now know the many causes of poor symmetry, but how can it affect your horse? A story from my past might help you answer this important question. When I was younger, (and braver), my father asked me to go mountain climbing. Since I spent most of my time riding with girls he probably thought I needed to do something macho. We prepared for our trip a few days in advance, with my father giving me the responsibility of organizing my own backpack. Unfortunately, I had no idea how to do this and put my pot, pan, silverware, small propane tank, and climbing gear on one side, and shoved my lightweight sleeping bag on the other. Immediately after we started to climb, it became painfully obvious to me that the unbalanced load I was carrying was horribly—and, on very steep terrain at 12,000 feet, dangerously—asymmetrical! I tripped and stumbled, had a difficult time turning in both directions, developed a short stride and limp, and felt one side of my body stiffen and become sore. In addition to these uncomfortable and painful physical symptoms, I was also feeling distracted, frustrated, and short-tempered. Who would have believed that something like a little pack could have such a profound effect on my *frame* and *frame of mind*? Who would believe that I could hate mountain climbing so much!

An unbalanced rider can have a very similar effect on her horse. Instead of an unbalanced pack, imagine how your horse feels when you ride with more weight on one seat bone and in one stirrup. Chances are pretty good that one or more of the following things will occur.

1. The horse contracts the muscles on one side of his body in order to carry you. As a result, he has difficulty bending his body on that side, remaining balanced through corners, picking up both leads, and moving in a straight line without drifting to one side.

2. He trips and stumbles more often than normal because of your unbalanced and shifting weight.

3. He develops a slight limp so that the hind leg that is supporting less weight can shift under and across his body to support his side with the heavier load. This also interferes with his ability to lengthen his stride and develop a regular rhythm. To understand how this might feel, think about how your body and stride is affected when you carry a saddle, or heavy feed bucket on one side of your body.

Can you walk in a straight line?

Imagine that you're going to a horse show in Africa and become stranded in the Sahara desert. With no landmarks in sight, you must walk in a perfectly straight line for 10 miles to reach the show grounds. You have plenty of food and water, and you routinely jog 10 miles a day. Do you think you can do it?

While this situation sounds easy, it may be difficult to walk a straight line—not because it's too hot or too far, but because the left and right side of your body are probably different. If one hip joint or leg is stiffer or weaker, there's a chance that its stride will be shorter than the stronger, more flexible side. Without any points of reference, this imbalance will actually cause you to walk in a circle. You would most likely come across your own footprints after hours of walking in what you assumed was a straight line!

"The show grounds must be here... somewhere..."

Blind leading the blind

The next time you take a lesson, try this simple exercise to see if you ride as symmetrically as you think. (It's important to do this with an instructor present.) With your eyes open, walk or trot in a straight line down the middle of the arena while focusing on a point directly in front of you. Once completed, repeat the same move, only this time with your eyes closed. In the beginning, close your eyes for a few strides only, and have your instructor tell you if you're about to ride out of the arena. If you ride with more weight in one seat bone or stirrup, your horse will likely move in that direction even though you may feel as if you're riding straight.

Another technique to practice is riding without complete use of your reins. Again, only try this with a riding teacher who agrees that you're ready. While walking or trotting down the center of the ring, grab the reins in the center only (on the buckle) and stop steering with your hands and legs. If you're asymmetrical, your horse will likely start to drift off to one side.

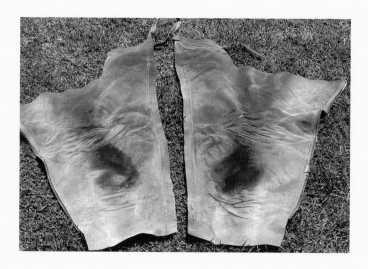

2.7 Signs of Asymmetry

It's obvious from the wear—wrinkles and color of the leather—that the owner of this pair of chaps rides with more right leg contact.

4. He becomes confused, distracted, frustrated, and angry because of the conflicting body, leg, and rein aids coming from your asymmetrical body.

5. He feels pain, discomfort, and physical fatigue on the side of his body that is supporting more weight. It's not uncommon for veterinarians or equine massage therapists to notice these symptoms on only one side of a horse's body.

Signs of Rider Asymmetry

As mentioned, imperfect rider symmetry can have a very negative effect on the horse. For this reason, it's important that you remain as symmetrical as possible whenever you ride. To do this, you first need to find out if your body has asymmetrical tendencies. There are several unmounted exercises in Chapter Six that help you accomplish this, but you can learn a lot by simply looking at your tack, body, clothing, and riding habits to see if they tell you something. If you notice any of the following signs, there's a good chance you're asymmetrical.

1. One stirrup leather is stretched more than the other, or you have uneven wear marks on your rubber stirrup pads.

2. Your saddle, or saddle pad, constantly slips to one side when you ride.

Your body is like a shopping cart

At least once, you've probably had to push around a grocery store shopping cart that went less than perfectly straight. Maybe a front wheel was crooked or a back wheel was stuck, and no matter how hard you tried, the shopping cart refused to go straight. You probably corrected the problem by steering it in the opposite direction, and the result of your counteraction was that the cart usually went straight.

Your body can act much like this shopping cart. If you asymmetrically place more weight in one seat bone or leg, your horse will likely think you want him to move toward that side. Your hands, however, can make him go straight by steering him slightly to the opposite side. Just like the shopping cart, your counteracting aids (body versus hands) can convince your horse to go straight, but only after your body tells him left and your hands tell him right, thus causing him some degree of confusion, frustration, and discomfort. Learn to make your shopping cart (and horse) move well in a straight motion by making sure that your front and back wheels (body and hands) are symmetrical and straight!

3. You have "wear" marks on *one* side of your saddle, boots, britches, gloves, chaps, or saddle pad (fig. 2.7).

4. Your boots, britches, or chaps pinch, or cause some other form of discomfort, on one leg or hip, and not the other.

5. Your legs suffer from rub marks in different locations or varying severity.

6. You continually need to tuck your shirt into one side of your pants, or your shirt frequently slides down one shoulder.

7. You carry one hand higher or one shoulder lower.

8. One foot (or leg) cramps or falls asleep, while the other feels normal.

9. The stitching or leather on one rein rubs more or weakens faster.

10. You constantly twist your head or look in one direction.

11. Your helmet falls to one side or presses uncomfortably on one side of your neck.

12. You unconsciously re-center your saddle by pushing your weight into one stirrup after halting.

13. When you fall, you always fall off on the same side.

It's my experience that most cases of asymmetry start with an imbalance in the hip area and spread throughout the rest of the body. For instance, if your hips shift to the left: your torso will collapse on the right, more weight will be placed on your left seat bone and leg, your right shoulder will drop, and your left hand will rise. In an attempt to offset this shift in balance, you may unconsciously extend your right arm and drop your head to the right. This is your body's way of trying to rebalance itself. If your hips have caused a 10-pound shift to the left, you may unconsciously open your right arm (5 pounds to the right) and drop your head to the right (another 5 pounds to the right) to offset the imbalance. While your body may believe the situation has been remedied, it's actually only complicated it by adding muscular tension and torsion to the already existing problem of poor symmetry.

One of the most effective ways to diagnose asymmetry is to listen to your body. When I was 19, I was invited to ride in Ireland for two

Ask yourself a question

Do you prefer carrying a 10-pound feed bucket in one hand, or two 7-pound feed buckets—one in each hand? Chances are you prefer carrying the two buckets (even though they're heavier) because the weight is symmetrical and it balances your body. I'm sure your horse feels the same way.

2.8 A & B *Stephanie finds it easier to carry two heavy buckets that balance each other out than it is to carry one on its own.*

months. I was excited because Irish horses are some of the most talented in the world. In preparation for my trip, I purchased a pair of custom chaps. After a few weeks, I noticed a few small holes appearing in the right leg of the chaps. Initially, I blamed this on poor material, but later decided that it was easier to blame the horses.

At about this time, I also began to notice a weird coincidence. All the horses in Ireland seemed to be stiff on the right. I felt as if they

Test your symmetry (1)

Find out if your body has asymmetrical tendencies by trying this simple test. Place two identical bathroom scales on a solid floor and stand so one foot is on each (avoid using two different types of scales because it may reduce the test's accuracy). Bend your knees, shift your weight onto your heels, and place your hands in front of your body as if holding a pair of reins. Wait a few seconds to let the scales record their weights, and then have a helper write down the two separate results. Don't look down at the scales as this will cause your weight to shift forward and alter the readings. If one scale records more weight, there's a good chance your body is asymmetrical.

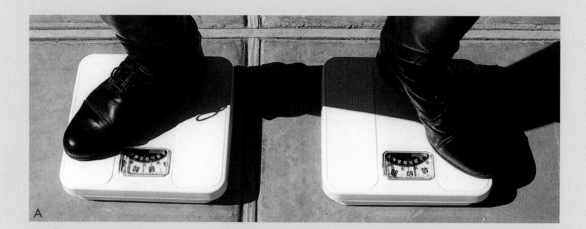

2.9 A & B

Even though this rider was trying to put even weight on both scales, you can see that in A, she placed more weight on her right leg. In B, a slight shift is all it took for her to balance out her stance.

were all bred to run in one direction around an island-sized racetrack! By the end of my trip, I'd not only worn large holes in the right leg of my chaps, I had no hair left on the inside of my lower right leg, either. When I returned home, I told my coach about Irish horses all being stiff on the right. Without hesitation, he told me, in no uncertain terms, that I was an idiot because I was the one who was stiff on the right. While at first I didn't believe him (after all, I was a typical young man who could do no wrong), I learned to trust his words as my body awareness started to improve. Today, I can only imagine how much more enjoyable my Irish experience would have been if I had only paid attention to the obvious signs and listened to what my own body was trying to tell me.

Asymmetry in Horses

Horses also suffer from asymmetrical tendencies, and like us, their problems start at birth and are exaggerated by behavioral factors. As a result of the shape of the equine fetus in the womb, a foal develops a dominant side well before birth. Later, you accentuate any asymmetrical tendencies by approaching, mounting, leading, and caring for the horse on his left side. While this "equine etiquette" certainly makes you less threatening to him by being predictable, these habits increase the imbalance of his body by making his left side stiffer and stronger than his right. This may be why your horse prefers one lead, or has an easier time turning in one direction. You can tell if your horse has a dominant side by watching him grazing. If he's asymmetrical, he extends the same leg forward each time he lowers his head to eat (fig. 2.10).

Conclusion

Horses and riders suffer from imperfect symmetry. Until you're certain you're symmetrical, you can't be sure that your body isn't causing your horse to be unbalanced. Imagine how difficult it is to help a horse that's stiff on his left if you continually place more weight on that side of his body. When you become symmetrical, you have the self-confidence, skill, coordination, and balance needed to help your horse overcome his problems.

Since your asymmetrical tendencies aren't created by riding, you won't need your horse to solve them. Remember, it's not a horse-and-rider problem, it's simply a problem born out of being right- or left-handed, which is then

2.10 Dominant Side

When grazing, a horse puts his dominant leg forward (to support his weight) as he moves ahead.

Test your symmetry (2)

Next time you ride, make sure your saddle and pad are placed evenly on your horse's back. Do this by having someone hold the reins and balance your horse on all four legs while you check to see that saddle and pad are centered. Ride for a while, then dismount softly, being careful not to drag the saddle to the left. Have your helper balance your horse again, then look to see if your saddle and pad have shifted to the left or right. If the answer's yes, you are riding asymmetrically. Remove your saddle pad, turn it over and examine the dirt, hair, and sweat on it. If the wear pattern is asymmetrical, so are you.

magnified by your behavioral patterns. Trying to solve these while mounted may be impossible (after all, you'd have corrected them a long time ago if it were that easy) so a little time spent on self-improvement away from your horse may be just what the doctor ordered. Self-improvement exercises in between your riding sessions should be considered every bit as important as the time you actually spend in the saddle. You need to perform a variety of unmounted exercises to improve the left and right balance of your body, and equalize your coordination, strength, stamina, and flexibility. Once you've found your new symmetry, don't be surprised if many of your horse's problems miraculously disappear.

CHAPTER THREE

BALANCE

When you are perfectly balanced, you can remain relaxed in the saddle and encourage your horse to move in a purposeful and economical manner. As soon as your balance is compromised, your ability to *Ride Right* and communicate with your horse is lost. Getting "left behind" during a canter depart, falling inward during a turn, and landing on your horse's neck after a jump are three good examples of how poor balance can affect your horse's movements. Your unintentional "motions" become incorrect aids that distract and confuse your horse, cause him discomfort, and limit his performance.

As I discussed earlier, there's a point in your body, called your *center of gravity*, that's the very center of your mass. This is also your *center of balance* when riding. If you were to separate your body into equal halves along the horizontal, front-vertical, and side-vertical planes, the lines would intersect at this spot. Due to variations in body shape and size, the center of gravity changes from person to person but is usually located deep in the pelvic region.

The lower your center of gravity, the more naturally balanced you are. You can test this by standing with feet shoulder-width apart, and bending your knees. Since your center of gravity is closer to the ground, you'll feel very

"There... ten pads should make you nice and comfy."

3.2 *Even though the rider thinks she is being kind, she's going to raise her center of balance with all these pads and make her horse uncomfortable as a result of her loss of balance.*

3.1 Center of Gravity

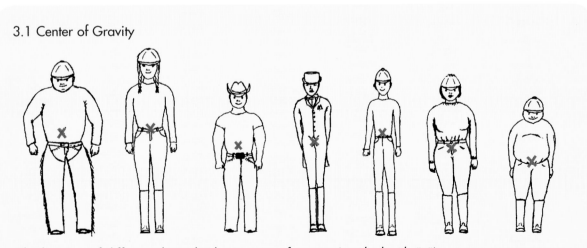

The location of different-shaped riders' center of gravity (marked with "x").

3.3 A & B High Center of Balance

Maria and Stephanie demonstrate a high center of balance: in photo A, there is a large gap between Maria's britches and the saddle, and in B, Stephanie falls forward in the saddle. Both indicate that balance is compromised when the center of gravity is not as low as possible.

balanced. Now straighten your knees, stand on your toes, and stretch your arms and body upward as high as possible. You'll feel less balanced in this position because you've taken your previously low center of gravity and elevated it (fig. 3.2).

To avoid balance problems while riding, keep your center of gravity as low as possible. Four ways to accomplish this are by moving your hips forward instead of upward during the posting trot, keeping your buttocks close to your saddle, placing your weight deep into your heels, and keeping your knees bent with your kneecaps facing slightly downward.

A second characteristic that influences your balance in the saddle is your *base of support*. This is the distance between your seat bones (for example, in the sitting trot), your inner thighs, or your feet (in the two-point position). The greater the distance between these points, the more balanced you'll be. Test this by standing with your feet wide apart and then with

your feet touching one another. Have a friend try to push you off balance in both positions. You'll have a much easier time maintaining your balance when this base of support is wide. You can widen it in the saddle by keeping your hips and inner thighs relaxed (imagine your skin is so supple it fills in all the nooks and crannies of your saddle), and your knees open. Pinching with your knees is a sure way to create balance problems because it decreases the distance between your two bases of support.

Raising your center of gravity causes your base of support to narrow. Imagine what your legs would look like if you were to post to the trot in an up-and-down manner instead of a forward-and-backward one. Each time you elevated your body, your knees (and hip bones) would squeeze together. Test this by standing on your toes in your stirrups as tall as possible, while holding the mane for balance. As you lift your body, you'll feel your knees (and hip bones) close toward one another (figs. 3.3 A & B).

Likewise, narrowing your base of support raises your *center of gravity*. Test this by sitting in your saddle with relaxed hips and thighs, then contract your buttock muscles (pulling your hip bones together), and feel your body move upward. Don't be surprised if you feel your knees pinch together as you squeeze your buttocks because narrowing the base of support of one body part almost always results in the narrowing of others.

In order to remain balanced, your center of gravity must also remain over your feet. Fall forward in the saddle (for example, collapse your body forward while jumping), and the shift in balance will cause your legs to slide backward (figs. 3.4 A & B). Fall backward (get left behind a canter depart or a jump), and your legs will slide forward (figs. 3.5 A & B). A badly balanced upper body is almost always responsible for poor leg position. Fix your upper body, and your legs will correct themselves (figs. 3.6 A–F and 3.7 A–D).

Consider the physical tension your body must generate to stabilize your body, and it's easy to see how this can affect your horse's balance, rhythm, and stride. You can test this by standing on your left leg and leaning forward. As you do, your right leg will swing backward. Bring your upper body back to a vertical position and your right leg will return to a relaxed position under your center of gravity.

Make your horse invisible

The next time you watch a rider, imagine that her horse is invisible. If she's standing comfortably, she's riding in balance. If she appears to be falling forward, her center of gravity is in front of her base of support; if she appears to be falling backward, it's behind her base of support.

Your center of gravity must also remain over your horse's center of gravity. Depending on his breed, discipline, and age, his center of gravity is likely located slightly behind his heart in the girth area. At birth, his center of gravity is far forward in his body, resulting in the term *built downhill*, but as he matures, his center of gravity shifts backward and he becomes *built uphill*, thanks to an increase in his back, torso, and hindquarters musculature (fig. 3.8).

The center of gravity of a horse participating in a sport (dressage, for instance) requiring hindquarter strength, a compact body, and a rounded neck is located far back in his body. The center of gravity of a horse participating

**When you ride with your eyes forward, you see your future.
When you ride with your eyes down, you see your immediate future!**

Regardless of your riding discipline, you should always look where you're going because it helps you maintain correct posture in turns and straight lines. Unfortunately, if you look down long enough, you might just be doing the same thing, that is, looking where you're going!

When you look down, your head shifts slightly forward. Since your body automatically adjusts itself whenever it feels a shift in balance, it equalizes the forward weight shift by moving some other part of your body backward. This is why riders who look down usually have a difficult time keeping their lower legs from sliding back.

3.4 A & B Too Forward Jumping Balance

In A, Hannah is positioned too far forward and her weight is out of balance. However, in B, her center of gravity is nicely balanced over her feet—she could stand on the ground in this position. Note the difference of her leg position in both photos.

3.5 A & B Too Backward Jumping Balance

In A, Lizzie's weight is too far backward. But in B, she has corrected her balance so if her horse suddenly disappeared from underneath her, she would land in a comfortable, standing-up position.

3.6 A–F Center of Balance

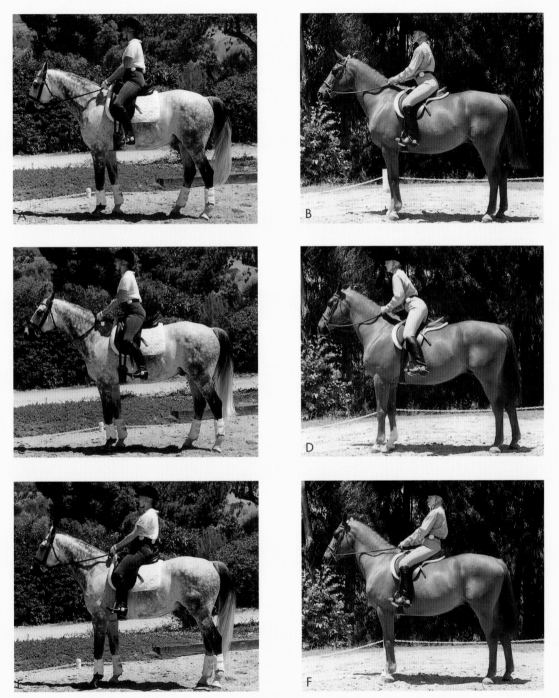

Note the yellow disks that the riders are wearing. Photos A and B show
riders with a correct center of balance in both dressage and jumping saddles.
C and D show the same riders when their center of balance has shifted
forward. See how their legs go back when this happens. In E and F their
center of balance is back, and their legs are now too far forward.

When a horse walks uphill, his center of balance shifts forward, and going downhill, it shifts back. In A and B, Mary-Jo is riding well and moving her center of balance forward and back over the top of Dusty's center of balance. In C and D, Mary-Jo and Dusty are not aligned. Consequently, neither horse nor rider looks balanced.

in a sport requiring a long body and lengthy, low neck (Western pleasure is an example) stays quite far forward; and that of the jumper is located somewhere in between the two. This is why dressage riders are taught to ride in a vertical position, and jumpers are taught to ride in front of the vertical. They're both doing something correct, and that's keeping their center of gravity directly over their horse's center of gravity (figs. 3.9 A–C).

Male and Female Balance

Men tend to have wide shoulders, narrowly spaced-apart hip bones, and long upper bodies—three characteristics that create a *high* center of gravity. Women tend to have narrow shoulders, widely spaced-apart hip bones, and lighter, shorter, upper bodies—three characteristics that create a *low* center of gravity. As a result, women usually win the prize when it comes to stability in the saddle. Men, if you've

3.8 The Horse's Center of Balance

As a horse's muscles develop, his center of gravity shifts further back, and he becomes more "built uphill."

been looking for an excuse, you've just found it! It's important to remember, however, that these are only generalizations, and there are exceptions to this rule (fig. 3.10).

One exception is a large-busted woman. Due to the heavy size and weight of her chest, her center of gravity is elevated and shifted forward, a condition that usually results in balance problems and lower-back discomfort. A second exception, with the *opposite* effect, occurs when a male rider eats or drinks too much, developing a large stomach that lowers his center of gravity.

I'm quite certain, though not particularly proud, that this is probably the only time you'll ever hear a sports therapist singing the praises of a "beer belly"! Seriously though, the health risks associated with this condition, not to mention the decrease in stamina, suppleness, and strength, far outweigh the benefits.

Are you built for balance?

The correlation between the height of your upper and lower body, and the width of your hips and waist dictates whether or not your body is *built for balance*:

1. The shorter your upper body, the lower your center of gravity, and the longer your legs, the better your leg contact will be.

2. The narrower your upper body and the wider your hips, the lower your center of gravity and the wider your base of support will be.

You're an animal!

The relationship between *base of support* and *center of balance* is evident in nature every minute of every-day. Your brain, as well as those of most animals, has an innate reflex to lower the center of balance and widen the base of support in a situation requiring stability. In nature, this is called the *fight or flight reflex* because animals naturally place themselves in the lower and wider position so they're better able to fight an attacker or take flight away from it. The next time you see your horse playing in the paddock, watch how he lowers his body and widens his stance when he turns a sharp corner. Your dog does the same thing when he plays with a ball by placing his front legs, paws, neck, and chin on the ground while leaving his hind end up in the air. Both of these animals are improving their balance by lowering their center of gravity and widening their base of support.

3. The ideal for riding is a short, light-weight, upper body, long legs, wide hips, and narrow shoulders.

To find out if your body is *built for balance*, compare the length of your upper body (UB) to the length of your lower body (LB). Do this by sitting on a table and having a friend measure the distance from the table to the top of your head (UB). Once you have this measurement, find the length of your lower

Notice how the horses' center of balance is different depending on the riding discipline. All riders, as in these drawings, must keep their center of balance aligned directly over their horse's.

Congratulations. Your horse just rolled on you!

I know a horse that rewards a balanced rider by rolling while she's still on his back. Like many horses, Kaoba adores scratching his sweaty belly after a vigorous lesson, and if his rider is well balanced during the cool-down, he forgets she's there, drops to his knees, and rolls over! If the rider loses her balance and shifts around in the saddle during the cool-down, he's reminded that she's still there and stays on all four feet. Kaoba compliments the rider by rolling because she becomes invisible to him!

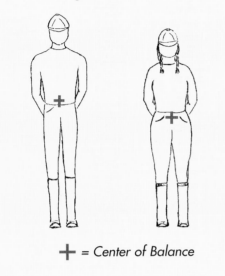

3.10 *Compare the center of balance in the average male and female.*

+ = Center of Balance

body by subtracting your upper body length from your overall height, and then divide the length of your lower body into the length of your upper body. You'll be left with a balance ratio you can compare to the benchmarks in the sidebar on this page. Place your calculations in the spaces provided, or in a notebook.

A second way to approximate whether you're *built for balance* is to divide your waist measurement by your hip measurement. Be sure to remove your clothing so it's not included in these measurements. Your hips should be larger than your waist, resulting in a total value of less than 1.0. The lower your score, the greater your chances of having a low *center of gravity* and wide *base of support*. For female riders, a score of 0.9 is considered good while a value of 0.8 or less is very good. Male riders tend to have narrower hips, and as a result may find that their scores are a little higher. Any value under 1.0 is considered good, while a score under 0.9 is very good.

Effects of Poor Balance on a Horse

Even though you may only weigh one-tenth as much as your horse, riding with poor balance can still cause him a number of problems. To help you understand why, imagine this situation: you're jogging through a park on a sunny day with your six-month old baby sleeping soundly in the baby carrier you have strapped to your chest. You have a nice long stride, rhythmical pace, perfect posture, easy breathing, and great agility. It's a great day and you feel good. You're able to completely focus on your jogging, and as a result, you can quickly and effortlessly adjust your stride and speed whenever you encounter dogs, children, and other joggers. You're in the zone. Your baby now wakes up. Instead of being still, she begins to wiggle around. She leans to her left and then right, throws herself forward to give you a hug, and then backward to take a good look at you. She reaches to her right to touch a dog, to her left to pull a leaf from a tree, and then takes hold of your lower lip and hair and gives them both a good yank. It's easy to see how the baby, one-tenth your weight, affects your *frame* and ability to jog comfortably. Well, so it is for a horse.

Posture

A properly aligned spine and symmetrical back are imperative for good posture because any misalignments you have on the ground

Test your balance

1. Stand with your knees slightly bent and your arms in front of your body as if holding a pair of reins.

2. Lift your right foot off the ground, place it behind your left knee, and balance on your left leg.

3. Close your eyes and remain balanced for as long as possible.* A friend should record the amount of time you are able to balance on your left foot (he should stop timing the second you open your eyes, or place your right foot on the ground). Once you open your eyes due to a loss of balance, reset yourself, and repeat the test a second time. Add both times together and divide the total by 2 to get the average balance time for your left leg. Repeat the same procedure while balancing on your right leg.

Results

If you have good balance, you'll be able to remain in the "blind" position for at least 30 seconds (at first it may be hard to hold it for more than a few seconds, but you'll improve quickly).

If your body is more balanced on one side, it indicates an asymmetry. Practice the test more on your unbalanced side so that you can bring your body into a more symmetrical balance.

* Stand beside a wall in case you get a little "wobbly." If you feel uncomfortable at any point, open your eyes and start over.

3.12 A & B Test Your Balance.

Keep your posture in line with these do's and don'ts

Do

Do use a mounting block when you can. It's easier on you and your horse's back.

Do sit up straight, and stand with your shoulders open.

Do stretch your chest, shoulders, back, buttocks, and hamstring muscles.

Don't

Don't use your back to pick up items (including when picking out horses' feet). Bend your knees and keep your back straight, letting your legs do the work.

Don't carry heavy items, such as your saddle or feed bucket, far from your body or always in the same hand.

Don't hold your breath when carrying heavy items.

are multiplied as soon as you sit on your horse. Your spine consists of 33 vertebrae, each one piled on top of another to form a slight "S" shape. A small flaw in any one of these vertebrae can affect the stability of your entire spinal column. When unbalanced or weak back muscles cause spinal instability, poor posture usually results. Imagine piling 33 bales of hay on top of one another. As long as the pile is perfectly balanced, it stands without effort, but try pulling a single bale from the middle of the pile, and it affects the stability and balance of the entire stack. This is what can happen to your posture if even one of your vertebrae becomes slightly displaced.

The only way to combat poor posture is to be sure that your back, chest, buttocks, and stomach muscles are symmetrically supple and strong. When you improve your overall posture, you'll be able to ride in a more relaxed, balanced, and symmetrical manner.

Don't be so pushy!

Are you unsure how easy it is for an unbalanced rider to affect the balance of a horse? If so, try this simple test. All you need is your horse and a friend.

Place your horse in cross-ties, and stand in front of him. Have your partner stand beside your horse's left hindquarter, gently place one index finger into his left rump, and using only that finger, slowly push him forward. As she does, watch your horse's chest muscles as they flinch and tighten. It's amazing how such a slight movement in the back of a horse can cause such a big reaction all the way in his front.

When a single finger can influence the balance and muscular tension of a horse weighing hundreds of pounds, it's proof enough that his body is sensitive to shifts in weight, including the shift that occurs when you lose your balance.

CHAPTER FOUR

BODY AWARENESS

The riding faults that are the most difficult to correct are those you are not aware of. Unless you are able to "feel" your mistakes you will keep repeating them. This knowledge of oneself is called *body awareness*, and it has a huge affect on your ability to *Ride Right* because you can't correct a mounted flaw unless you know it exists. Unfortunately, when you lack *body awareness*, it's possible to blame your horse for the flaws your own (unaware) body is creating.

In my introduction, I told you about a rider who had me videotape her horse in the hopes of finding out why he was so stiff on his right side. As you may recall, she'd asked her veterinarian, massage therapist, and farrier to try and find his problem, but wasn't able to solve it until she learned that she rides with more weight on her right seat bone and stirrup. I was able to solve her horse's problem by making her aware of how her body was affecting the body of her horse. This story demonstrated how a rider can, without knowing it, blame a horse for something her own body is causing. It also illustrates how a lack of body awareness can impede the future progress of both horse and rider. After all, if she hadn't been made aware of her flaw, she'd, no doubt, still be doing it today.

Videotapes and photographs can be a big help, but they're not a necessity when it comes to improving your body awareness. In fact, the easiest way to do so is simply by listening to your body. The better you become at translating your body's language, the better you'll ride. If this language remains foreign, both

"What's wrong with him? He feels so crooked, Doctor."

Congratulations! You're not perfect...

Every time I teach a clinic, I ask if there are any riders in the room who place more weight in one stirrup or seat bone when they ride. There are always a few brave souls who raise their hands. I always compliment these riders, because even though they admit to being imperfect, they obviously have a good sense of body awareness. After all, if they didn't, they wouldn't be able to recognize they are riding asymmetrically. The interesting thing is that even though only a handful of riders admit to this problem, other riders suffer from it but aren't aware of it. Who do you think has a better chance of correcting their imperfections, those who are aware or those who aren't?

you and your horse will have to struggle to *Ride Right*. When I was 13 years old, I took a crash course on the language of my body. I was the only boy at my barn, and I thought I was the smartest kid around. After all, the rest of the boys were playing football or baseball while I was constantly surrounded by droves of girls! Since I was the only boy, my ego often got in the way of listening to my instructor.

Body awareness is like learning to drive a car

During your first driving lesson, you're taught to stay relaxed and keep your eyes focused on the road in front of you. Once you get the hang of this, you're taught to monitor your position on the road by periodically checking the rear- and side-view mirrors. You can use these simple rules to improve your body awareness.

1. Focus forward on the riding task you're trying to accomplish, and,

2. Periodically, visualize looking in imaginary mirrors attached to your helmet so that you can "see" your position in the saddle. Try seeing things such as the amount of weight in each seat bone, the position of your shoulders, the tension in your hips, and the location of your hands.

For months, she told me that my legs were too far forward and kicking my horse's shoulders, but I was certain they were placed correctly just behind the girth. While her words entered my ears, they didn't get much further because I was too caught up in what a great rider I was. It wasn't until after my first show when I took a fall and another trainer told me it was caused by my poor leg position that I finally started to listen. I was so confident in my position that I had completely ignored what my own body was telling me. That day was one of the most influential in my entire riding career, because it was when I learned the importance of body awareness.

Body awareness also helps you understand the language of your horse. While he doesn't speak English or "rider," you still expect him to understand your language. Likewise, you don't speak "horse," but he has the right to expect you to understand his language as well. The only way you can do this is by listening as closely to his body as you do your own. At one time or another, you've probably felt the teeth-gritting frustration associated with riding a horse that seems intent on doing the opposite of everything you ask. The big, lovable animal that you just had to have suddenly becomes a crazy, hair-covered monster. Instead of appreciating his unique personality and quirkiness, you probably spend more time trying to figure out how to nail a *For Sale* sign to his tail. The only way to avoid this kind of frustration is to keep a positive attitude, and learn to understand what he's trying to tell you. To do this, you're going to need to develop your body awareness. It helps to speak "horse," too!

Recognize, Relay, Reflect, and Respond

Body awareness is a four-step program. The way in which your body *recognizes* information about itself (and the body of your horse), and the time taken to *relay* this information to your brain make up the first two steps. The speed at which your brain is able to *reflect* upon the information and then create a *response* to it, make up the last two steps. When your mind and body are proficient at *recognizing, relaying, reflecting,* and *responding,* you have a good sense of body awareness.

Recognize and Relay

Steps 1 and 2: the more quickly your body *recognizes* and *relays* information about your body and your horse's body to your brain, the more quickly your brain can decide what to do with it. The canter departure is a good example. When a *novice* rider asks for one, she must first wait for her horse to pick up the canter before she uses her eyes to see whether she's on the correct lead. This method of recognizing and relaying information is very slow. An *advanced* rider, on the other hand,

Listen to your body

The information your body sends to your brain comes from two sources:

1. Vestibular System A group of highly sensitive canals, ducts, hair-like processes, nerves, and sensors in your inner ear provides your brain with information about direction, rotation, body position, acceleration, and balance. While most novices usually only use this source when they're in the middle of saying, "Oops! I'm going to fall off now," advanced riders usually find many more useful ways of using their *vestibular system*.

2. Proprioceptors Every tendon, ligament, muscle, and joint capsule in your body contains supersensitive sites called *proprioceptors,* which are sensitive to movement, pressure, weight, stretch, and changes in position. The information gained from these sources travels up your spine to your brain, where it's interpreted and an appropriate response elicited. Important *riding receptors* in your body are found in your feet, calves, knees, inner thighs and hips, seat bones, hands, elbows, and shoulders.

Your eyes can also provide you with a wealth of information about your position, balance, and acceleration and more, but since vision is an external sense, it's not normally referred to as *body awareness*. While you may use your vision to see if your body has accomplished a goal (looking to see if you've picked up the correct canter lead, for example), it's unfortunately very slow, therefore relatively ineffective. Your goal as a rider is to hone your body awareness so that you don't have to rely on your eyes to tell you what your vestibular system and proprioceptors should have told you long ago.

actually *senses* her horse is going to pick up the correct lead seconds before she even starts to canter. A slight variation in the balance and rhythm of her horse's stride is all she needs to feel. Her body awareness, or something I like to call "horse sense," is so honed that she has no need of the slower sense of sight to tell her if she's completed her goal or not.

Reflect and Respond

Steps 3 and 4: Your brain *reflects* upon the information it's received from your body and creates an appropriate *response* to it. When there's *no time* between the reflect and respond steps, the resulting action is called a *reflex*. While these super-fast responses are essential for making quick adjustments to your body and that of your horse, they often lead to errors in judgment. Blaming your horse for being stiff on one side without first checking to see if you're sitting symmetrically, is a good example. When there's a *brief pause* between the reflect and response steps, the resulting action is called a *reaction*. This process is slower because a thought process is involved, such as when you're in an unfamiliar situation and must look back on previous experiences to help you decide how to act in the present.

Reflex

The faster you're able to *reflect* and *respond* to the information coming from your body or your horse, the faster you can make the

"Hey! Yanking on my mouth isn't going to help me relax, you know!"

Punishment and reward

Every time your horse does something correctly, your *reflex* or *reaction* must include a "reward" (thereby encouraging him to continue moving in a correct manner). Every time your horse does something incorrectly, your reflex or reaction must communicate your displeasure and discourage him from repeating the mistake. The word "punishment" is often used to describe this kind of command, but punishment should not mean submitting your horse to an aggressive or uncomfortable sensation. In fact, one of the most effective forms of punishment is simply withholding the reward. Take the canter depart, for example:

You ask for a left lead and your horse picks up that lead. You reward him by letting him canter on and give him a pat on the neck. Five minutes later, you ask him for a right lead, but he picks up the left lead again. This time, you punish him by bringing him back to a walk. Your punishment, in this case, was simply withholding the reward of letting him canter on.

Your horse is not going to do everything you ask him to do. He may not be capable, or just intent on making your day miserable, but, regardless of the reason, it's your job to help him improve by providing plenty of positive action to encourage or discourage his actions.

necessary adjustments. Unfortunately, since *reflexes* happen so quickly, you can't always guarantee your decision will be entirely appropriate. There's simply not enough time to decide whether the action you're about to take is the correct one. Automatically lifting your hands and pulling hard on your horse's mouth when he does something wrong is a good example of a reflex that is not appropriate. After all, has this reflex ever worked to calm your horse? It's safe to say that given a little more time to reflect, you would've acted in a more productive and less aggressive manner.

Suppressing *inappropriate* reflexes with more suitable ones is an important skill to develop. When you were a novice rider, you probably experienced a situation where your horse became strong and ran away with you. Your automatic reflex to this out-of-control situation was probably to grab with your legs and lean forward even though your instructor was telling you to lean back and relax. While leaning forward isn't a bad idea if you're trying to win the Kentucky Derby, it's not the best way to handle a strong horse. What you probably should have done, short of jumping off and "pulling the ripcord," was to reflect a little longer, listen to your instructor, and then respond correctly by leaning back and relaxing.

Does inflicting pain ensure success?

To answer this question, imagine the following situation. Using sign language, someone tells you to hop on one leg, rub your tummy, and smile. You don't "speak" sign language, so you don't understand the instructions. Do you think it will help you to better understand the instructions if she comes over to you and hits you with a stick? What if she jabs you in the ribs with a fork? Will that help?

Horses do not "speak human," so you must do all you can to help your horse understand your language. Simply inflicting pain when he fails to do so only results in him feeling confused, tense, and resentful.

The process of replacing inappropriate reflexes takes a considerable amount of time and effort. Every time your brain recognizes a movement (your horse running away with you, for example), it will try to respond by engaging its automatic reflex (leaning forward). When you feel that a reflex is inappropriate, you can teach your brain to override it, but this causes an increase in the time between the *reflect* and *response* stage (*reaction time*) because your brain must search for another response. Once it finds a more appropriate response, it can be saved in your brain's database for future use. In time, your brain will learn to instinctively override your old inappropriate reflex and replace it with this new response. The new response, called your *learned reflex*, will take the place of your original, inappropriate reflex.

Reaction

Reaction time, or the amount of time between the *reflect* and *response* phase of an action, is controlled by past repetition and familiarity. When a situation is familiar—one you've encountered before, your reaction can be fast

> ## Reflexes are like eating chocolate
> *You know eating chocolate isn't the best thing in the world, but the urge to eat it is often too automatic to stop, and like a reflex, not always the best decision.*

because past experience helps you to decide how to react in the present. In the previous example, your first experience with a runaway horse almost killed you because you reacted without thinking. Later in your riding career, you learn to lean back and relax, but only after thinking about your instructor's words and recalling how leaning forward almost caused you to go "dirt-surfing." Thanks to this small hesitation (your *reaction time*), you no longer lean forward because your past experiences have taught you that it's the incorrect way to respond. Once you've experienced a situation such as this enough

Riding with reflexes and reactions

Your horse speeds up so you instinctively lean forward, become tense, and grab with your legs. You reason that falling won't hurt as much if you can just get yourself a little closer to the ground. As a result of this "fetal-position" reflex, your horse goes even faster. Your instructor screams at you to lean back and relax. You yell, "Yeah right!"

- You continue leaning forward and hanging on in fear for your life (not so much from falling anymore but from your irate instructor), until you finally listen to her and try leaning back. Your horse automatically relaxes and slows to a walk.

- The next time your horse gets out of control, your brain recalls its first reflex, discards it as inappropriate, and instead of repeating it, takes a few seconds to decide that the best way for you to respond is by leaning back and relaxing. As a result, your horse relaxes and slows to a walk. This *short reaction time* may have delayed your response slightly but will help you make important decisions more quickly and correctly in the future.

- The next time you encounter this situation, your *reaction time* will be even shorter. Before long, this short pause will disappear altogether, and your reaction will actually become a new reflex replacing your old inappropriate one.

times, your reaction time will become so fast that it'll actually disappear, and your reaction will become a reflex.

Your reactions are considerably slower when you're confronted with a situation that's unfamiliar to you. Since you've never rehearsed it, you're left with nothing but your instincts to guide you. Your brain must then ask itself three important, yet time-consuming questions, including, "What are my instincts telling me to do," "What are the consequences of this action," and "Is this really the best decision I can make?" Understandably, this conscious process is going to take time, but if it gives you the chance to make an intelligent decision, then the time will have been well spent. In fact, a well thought-out reaction is much better than an inappropriate reflex any day.

However, you should always try to decrease the duration of your reaction time. A jumper approaching a fence is a good example of how important fast reaction times need to be. As he nears the jump, he must judge, or "spot," the distance to it. Once he's done this, he can quickly calculate the number of strides it'll take to get there, and even shorten or lengthen his horse's stride to ensure that he arrives at the perfect take-off spot. While a talented jumper doesn't need much time to spot this distance, a less experienced rider often doesn't have enough time to decide where to take off. Unfortunately, by this time it's usually too late. As a result, novice jumpers are often forced to take off from a long spot, or "chip-in" an extra stride before the jump (fig. 4.3).

Coordination

A physical attribute that has a major affect on your ability to respond quickly and correctly to difficult riding situations is *coordination*. You're considered coordinated if you're able to perform a series of intricate riding movements correctly, smoothly, and gracefully in a short amount of time. Your ability to recognize, relay, reflect, and respond is greatly improved when you have coordinated control of your body. Without it, you'll have a diffi-

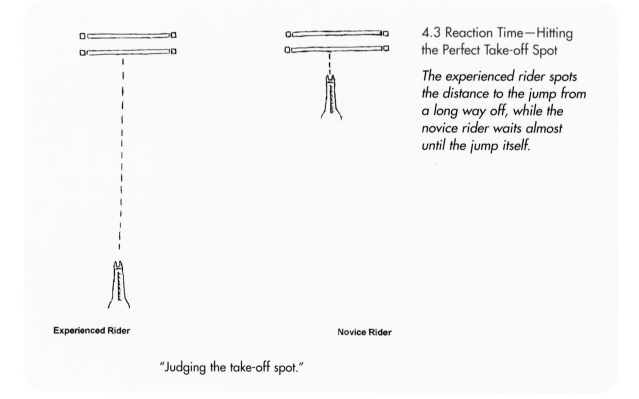

4.3 Reaction Time—Hitting the Perfect Take-off Spot

The experienced rider spots the distance to the jump from a long way off, while the novice rider waits almost until the jump itself.

Experienced Rider

Novice Rider

"Judging the take-off spot."

cult time developing the skill, speed, and confidence necessary to perform complicated and repetitive riding movements and adapt to your horse's ever-changing behavior. Remember, horses are like very complicated "people": one day they may love you, adore flapping plastic bags on the trail, and enjoy cantering on the correct lead, while the next, they'd rather be tube-wormed than deal with you, your plastic bags, or the correct leads! The more quickly and correctly you're able to act and react to their peculiar behavior, the better chance you'll have of riding well as a team.

*

Test your awareness

Repeat the symmetry-scales test (p. 22), only this time, stand with one foot on each scale and shift your weight right and left until you feel you have the same amount of weight on each scale. Now ask your partner to record the weights on each scale. If you have good body awareness, the scales will be equal. If the scales are recording a different weight, slowly shift your hips over to the lighter side until they are equal. You're now standing with the same amount of weight in each foot, even if it no longer feels like it.

To improve your body awareness, you need to overcome *muscle memory:* you've probably been standing for so long with more weight on one foot that you've convinced your unequal muscles they're equal! To reset your muscle memory, perform the scales test until the day you find that your body and the scales are telling you that you're in a balanced position. Once you achieve this, your incorrect muscle memory will have been replaced by your new and improved muscle memory. You'll now have an easier time recognizing and correcting your imperfections, thanks to your improved body awareness.

CHAPTER FIVE

BREATHING

All riders regardless of age, discipline, or skill level, hold their breath from time-to-time. You may do it because you simply forget to breathe during stressful riding situations or because you feel it gives you an added boost of strength. Whatever your reason, one thing is clear: holding your breath while riding *always* increases muscular tension in your body. Unfortunately, when this happens, your horse also feels the tension created by you. After all, if he can feel a fly land on him, he can certainly feel your body weight tense up while you're sitting on his back.

A long time ago, I owned a wonderfully talented mare, and I enjoyed almost every minute we spent together. The only exception was when we encountered a plastic bag blowing across the ring or down the trail. She would get spooked and bolt. What confused me most about her "spooks" was that she only seemed to do them when I was on her back. When my instructors rode her, she was as solid as a rock. After a while, this really started to bother me, especially on Mondays and Thursdays since they were "trash days" at my barn (imagine all the bags!) In an attempt to figure out why she was so spooky with me, my instructor suggested that he and I go for a ride

> ## Did you know?
>
> *A horse's resting respiration rate is about the same as ours—averaging 12 breaths per minute. His normal resting heart rate, however, is much lower than ours, only about 26 to 44 beats a minute. If his heart rate is as high as most riders, 60 to 80 for example, you should consider calling your vet. More than 80 beats per minute is a sign that something is seriously wrong.*

together. It didn't take long before he found the problem. Every time I saw a bag in the distance, I would anticipate the spook, prepare myself by taking in a big gulp of air and hold my breath until we passed it. This caused my body to become, as my instructor so eloquently stated, "crispy, like a piece of overcooked bacon." "Of course I'm tense," I told him, "I'm sure Chela's about to spook." "You're right," he agreed, "how can she remain calm when you're so darn spooked?" Chela wasn't spooking at the plastic bags, she was spooking

How long can you hold your breath?

To demonstrate how holding your breath can increase muscular tension, try this simple test. Stand in a riding position, take in a big deep breath, and hold it for as long as comfortably possible. During this time, ask yourself if your muscles are starting to tighten, if your shoulders start to rise, your hands begin to make fists, your knees start to pinch, and your back begins to hunch. Once it's no longer comfortable to hold your breath, exhale and immediately ask yourself if you feel a rush of relaxation flood through your body. Did your shoulders drop, hands open, and muscles relax? If you're like most riders, the answer to these questions is yes.

at me spooking at the plastic bags! All along, I thought I was reading her mind, but as it turned out, she was actually reading mine.

One way to avoid holding your breath during stressful riding situations is to *verbalize*. There's no way you can hold your breath while speaking; you must constantly inhale and exhale. Your talking can be made up of simple words, numbers, letters, even songs, although you should probably avoid singing if your voice is so bad (like mine) that it causes your horse more stress than the situation itself! I recently taught a clinic to a group of Pony Clubbers, and when I asked them, "How do you avoid holding your breath?" they all responded by singing the song, *Row-row-row-your boat!* I loved this answer because, not only does it ensure good breathing, it also helps establish a great sense of rhythm and tempo.

When it comes to using your voice as a breathing aid, why settle for one positive result when you can have several? In addition to good breathing, there are three things that talking, counting, and singing can do for your riding.

1. You can establish tempo by singing or repeating words or numbers in a rhythmical manner. Simple phrases such as "one-two," or a song phrase like "row-row-row your boat," are very effective because they have an intrinsic rhythm to them. When counting, use only numbers between 1 and 6 because they all have one syllable. Seven and 17 contain two

or more syllables and interfere with the rhythm of your verbalizations. The same rule goes for song phrases. When possible, only choose those that have the same number of syllables in each word.

2. Select words, numbers, or songs that deliver a verbal riding aid. Choose words that sound like a cluck, kiss, or whoa. "Tick-tock" can be used as a verbal aid for impulsion by simply placing a hard emphasize on each letter "T," thus making the words sound like a cluck or a kiss. Likewise, a phrase like "ho-hum" can be used as a calming aid by changing the inflection of the phrase from "ho-hum," to "whoa-hum." You already use the word "whoa" to calm your horse, so adding the word "hum" establishes a sense of rhythm. By the way, phrases like *"oh-no!"* or *"please stop!"* may not be the best choices when it comes to maintaining a calm and positive attitude.

3. Your words, numbers, or songs can have a calming effect on you and your horse if they become *white noise*. If you're not familiar with this term, it's a kind of nondescript background noise that takes the sharp edge off your concentration so that you can focus or relax more easily. I remember when I was teaching in New York City, I had to turn on a ceiling fan in order to get to sleep. It's calming

buzz helped draw my attention away from the horns, car alarms, and sirens blaring outside my window. The noise from a dishwasher, rain, or even the static on a television are all great sources of white noise. So, while riding, create your own white noise and select words, numbers, or songs that help you focus on your riding and not on all the other things occurring around you.

Chest and Diaphragm Breathing

There are two ways to breathe, and I don't mean just "in" and "out." Since proper breathing sharpens your mental focus, helps alleviate stress, improves your balance and posture, and provides your hard working muscles with plenty of oxygen, it's in your best interest to know what they are.

If your chest expands and your belly lies flat while breathing, you're a *chest breather*. While this type of breathing is the most common, it's unfortunately also the most ineffective. Since the majority of oxygen exchanges between your lungs and blood occurs in the lower region of your lungs, the energy used to send it "upstairs" is often wasted. Another consequence of chest breathing is that it causes your upper torso to expand and lengthen, which results in an increase in upper body tension and an elevated center of gravity. Suppleness,

Your nose knows

Your nose is very vascular and comes equipped with many tiny hairs. As a result, it can filter, heat, and humidify the air passing through it. Since your mouth is less efficient at performing these functions, the best way to breathe is by inhaling through your nose and exhaling through your mouth. This is especially true if you ride in a dusty arena or in cold, dry climates.

balance, and posture problems may plague your riding if you breathe this way.

If your stomach expands and your chest remains still while breathing, you're a *diaphragm breather*. Your diaphragm is a large muscle that separates your chest from your abdominal cavity. When it descends inside your body, it creates a vacuum that draws air into your lungs. This kind of breathing requires only about one-half as much energy as chest breathing. Additionally, diaphragm breathing doesn't contribute to upper body tension, or an elevation in your center of gravity.

Let your breathing stabilize your lower back

Each time you inhale using your diaphragm, imagine a balloon blowing up inside your stomach. As it inflates, it exerts slight pressure on the front of your spinal column, causing your lower back to feel more stable and supported. As a result, you'll use less effort and ride for longer periods of time without back fatigue.

5.1 *Imagine that as you breathe in, you inflate a balloon, which causes your stomach wall to expand and support your lower back.*

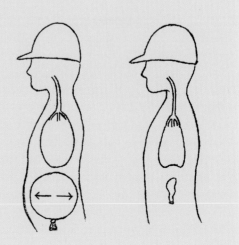

Test your breathing

Are you a *chest breather* or a *diaphragm breather?* Find out by taking this simple test. In a standing position, place one hand on your belly and the other on your chest. Inhale normally, and feel for movement in your upper and lower hand. If your upper hand moves the most, you're a *chest breather,* and if the lower hand moves the most, you're a *diaphragm breather.*

If you're a chest breather, take a few seconds to see if you can breathe using your diaphragm by expanding your stomach each time you inhale.

Once you can breathe using your diaphragm, try this second test. Stand with your hands on your waist so that your fingers are facing forward and your thumbs are facing backward. Perform a few diaphragm breaths, feeling your fingers expand toward the front wall. This should be easy. Now perform a few more breaths, and ask yourself if you can feel your thumbs expanding toward the back wall. This is going to be more challenging because your rigid, spinal column reduces the amount of movement you'll be able to feel. Concentrate, and you should be able to feel your thumbs expand toward the back wall adding support to your spinal column.

5.2 A & B Holding Your Breath

In A, Stephanie has taken in a big gulp of air and is holding it. Notice how tense her body has become—you can see it in her shoulders. In B, she has exhaled and is breathing normally with her diaphragm. You can see the difference in her body, which is now relaxed.

Posture and Breathing

Posture plays an important role in effective breathing. Every time you tilt your head up, down, to one side, or jut your chin forward, you inhibit the freedom with which air can enter your lungs. You can avoid this problem while riding by lengthening the back of your neck and keeping it in line with your spine. The best way I've found to accomplish this is by imagining you have a ponytail and someone is pulling on it in an upward motion. If done correctly, the back of your neck will stretch slightly, your chin will drop and soften, your shoulders will open, your chest will move forward, and your lower back will flatten. You now have a wonderful riding posture and your airway is completely opened and relaxed.

Test yourself to see if you can feel greater breathing freedom by thrusting your chin forward, closing your mouth, and breathing deeply through your nose. You'll likely feel and hear a resistance to the air passing from your nose down your throat. Now, lengthen the back of your neck as if someone is pulling upward on your ponytail, drop your chin, relax your mouth, and breathe deeply again through your nose. This time the air descending in your throat is doing so with much less resistance.

CHAPTER SIX

"EQUI-LIBRIUM" ENHANCING EXERCISES

Now that I've explained the importance of the four attributes necessary for a capable riding position: *symmetry, balance, body awareness,* and *breathing,* it's time for me to introduce some unmounted exercises that focus on improving you in these areas. You'll also achieve something I like to call "equi-librium." While the word ordinarily means balance or stability, my equi-librium means "complete balance between horse and rider." Your horse becomes more balanced because you've become more balanced, more symmetrical because you've become more symmetrical, and so forth.

The Key to Rider-Specific Exercises

The Stable Board

To perform many of the exercises in this book, you need a flat, wobbly surface to imitate and exaggerate the movements of the horse and rider. There is a special board designed for riders that I recommend, called the *Stable Board*

Principles of rider-specific exercise

Unmounted exercises will improve your mounted performance if they:

1. Imitate the movement of the horse and rider.

2. Exaggerate the most complicated physical challenges of riding.

3. Develop the strength, stamina, and suppleness of the muscles used while riding.

4. Are safe and enjoyable (if you feel comfortable and enjoy doing them there's a good chance you'll continue).

5. Are convenient. Having to join a gym or purchase expensive equipment decreases your motivation. Equipment should fit easily into your tack trunk. In addition, most of the exercises are designed to be done while standing. Having to lie down and sit on a tack room floor, or on the ground, only decreases your chances of doing them.

The equipment you need to do my exercises will fit into a tack trunk, so there is no need to join a health club.

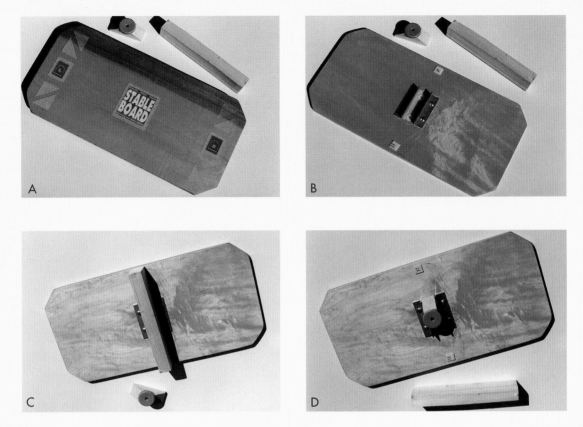

Photos A and B show the top and bottom surfaces, together with the attachments. C shows the large attachment in place, and D, the small attachment. To begin, use the large attachment. Once an exercise becomes easy, you can graduate to the small attachment. Warning: whenever you perform jumping exercises, use the large attachment only.

(figs. 6.2 A–D). I prefer the *Stable Board* because:

1. There are two attachments with each *Stable Board*: a *large, rectangular attachment* that causes the board to tilt left and right (easier), and a *small, round attachment* that causes the board to tip and rotate in every possible direction (difficult).

2. There are left and right stirrups painted on the top of each *Stable Board* so that you know exactly where to place your feet for precise balance and symmetry (see *Resources*, p. 168).

Unmounted Exercise Rules

In order for unmounted exercises to solve mounted problems and be called "rider specific," they must meet special criteria. Sport specificity is important to the development of any athlete and riders are no exception. While a general self-improvement program can help get you in shape, it lacks unique qualities needed to transfer the actual exercise benefits to your riding. In fact, some fitness and self-improvement programs, such as those that use "push-ups" to develop "stiff" chest muscles and "rounded" shoulders, may even harm

Pick a partner

You can perform rider-specific exercises on your own or with a partner (fig. 6.3). To start, perform exercises with a partner so that she can help you improve your body awareness by pointing out imperfections in your balance, symmetry, and breathing. Have her stand in front of you with her hands extended forward at waist height, and grasp her index fingers as if they're a pair of reins—without holding on to them for balance. Apply "educated contact" to her fingers so that she can feel how your hands respond to the challenges of the exercise. Her "movement-sensitive" hands will now take the place of your horse's movement-sensitive mouth. Instead of him telling you you're pulling on his mouth, she'll now be doing it.

When a partner isn't available, try performing the exercises in front of a full-length mirror so that you can see your imperfections for yourself (figs. 6.4 A & B).

6.3 *The partner is keeping his hands low and not crowding the rider on the Stable Board.*

6.4 A & B *When working alone, use a mirror. First, place your hands on the mirror's surface until you feel balanced. Once you are comfortable, close your fingers around imaginary reins.*

your riding performance. The exercises in this book have been designed with five very important principles in mind:

1. When performing rider-specific exercises, you must always imitate your *normal riding position*. Three examples:

- If you're a *jumper*, you should turn your feet slightly outward, place your weight in your heels, bend and open your knees, flatten your lower back, open your shoulders, and extend your arms well in front of your body with your elbows slightly bent and by your sides.

- If you're a *dressage* rider, your feet should be facing forward, your knees open but bent less than a jumper, your upper body tall, and your arms extended in front of your body with your elbows well bent and away from your sides.

6.5 Safety First!

Whenever you lean against a wall while on the Stable Board, always have a partner put a foot against the board so that it doesn't slip out from underneath you.

- The *Western* rider who neck-reins should imitate his regular riding position by dropping one arm to his side and extend the other arm in front of his body as if bridging the reins in that hand. Your *normal riding position* depends entirely on your riding discipline.

So that I can address all types of riders, from this point on, I'll refer to your specific exercise posture as your "*normal riding position.*"

2. When doing the exercises, listen carefully to what your body "tells" you, because they've been designed to exaggerate your mounted inadequacies or faults. In other words, when riding, if you hold your breath, place more weight on one foot, pinch with your knees, and lean forward, you'll do the very same things, only more pronounced, while exercising on the board. While this observation may sound cruel, it's actually very positive because it helps you locate your body's faults. Once your *body awareness* is able to feel your flaws, you'll have no trouble improving—just correct what your body's telling you, and practice the exercises until you notice improvement.

3. Always perform the exercises as perfectly as possible. If you get lazy and do them improperly, your body may become convinced that the wrong way is actually the right way. Once this happens, you'll have a difficult time persuading your body to change what you've already taught it.

4. Unless you like the taste of hospital food and enjoy having people sign your cast, make sure your exercise location is free of hazards! Tack rooms, wash-rack areas, and aisles are fine locations for your unmounted exercises, but only if they're free of tack and don't have slippery floors and nails sticking out of the walls. Also, for safety, always work with a partner when on the *Stable Board* and leaning against a wall. You need the help to prevent the board from slipping out underneath you (fig. 6.5).

5. Before starting an exercise program, check with your doctor. While rider-specific

exercises aren't overly taxing, it's always a good idea to get a thorough checkup. This is especially true if you have a history of health issues such as diabetes, heart disease, obesity, or high blood pressure.

Five "Equi-Librium" Exercises

As mentioned earlier, these exercises have been designed to improve your *symmetry*, *balance*, *body awareness*, and *breathing*. They may seem very challenging in the beginning but will quickly get more easy. In fact, don't be surprised if you find them much easier after only one day of practice. Does this mean that it only takes one day to fix all your symmetry, balance, body awareness, and breathing flaws? When I'm given the goals to achieve with a horse, I can expect my work to last anywhere from six weeks to six years. Obviously, it's going to take you a lot longer than one day to correct things a horse needs years to complete. While you may feel more balanced and symmetrical the next day, the improvement is most likely due to an overnight refinement in your body awareness.

Is that smoke coming from your legs?

During this, and many other Stable Board exercises, your leg muscles may begin to burn. Don't feel bad. This is a very normal reaction and actually helps your muscles improve. Unless you're feeling a sharp or shooting pain, try not to give up. Soon your muscles will become more fatigue-resistant and you'll notice less burning.

EXERCISE ONE
The Riding Lesson

Using the *large, rectangular attachment*, stand on your *Stable Board* so that one foot covers each stirrup mark (figs. 6.6 A & B). (If you use a different balance board, be sure that your feet are spread wide and at an equal distance from the center of the board. If one foot is closer to the center, it'll cause the board to tilt and affect the accuracy of the exercise.) Once your feet are placed evenly on the board, find your balance and assume your *normal riding position*.

6.6 A & B Riding Position

Note how Stephanie's feet are correctly equidistant from the center of the board in the normal riding position and the two-point position.

6.7 A & B Sitting Trot

The hips should be moved in both directions as Stephanie is doing here to the right, to imitate the motion of the sitting trot.

1. *The walk.* Start by moving your body in a way that mimics the motion of the horse's walk. Imagine placing equal weight in each seat bone, extend your hands forward as if confidently holding the reins, let each hip move forward in time with your horse's hips (visualize the movement of the agitator arm inside a washing machine), and wrap your legs around the sides of your horse without pinching your knees. Keep your weight in your heels, your knees open, eyes looking forward, and breathe rhythmically. Continue "walking" in this manner for one minute.

2. *The sitting trot.* Position yourself so that your back is flat, shoulders are open, knees bent, with weight in your heels. Slowly move your hips in an up-and-down motion (visualize the motion of a slow, sewing-machine needle), and move each hip forward in time with your horse's hip, much as you did at the walk. Continue for one minute (figs. 6.7 A & B).

3. *The posting trot.* From the sitting-trot position, stop all up-and-down motion, shift your hips backward, hold for a split second, and then shift them forward again. Each time you repeat this front-and-back motion, keep your knees bent and your weight in your heels (visualize the front-and-back motion of doing the hula-hoop). Again, do this for one minute (figs. 6.8 A–C).

4. *The canter.* Assume a position similar to the sitting trot, only instead of moving up-and-down, think of your hips as ice cream scoops removing ice cream from a carton. Your knees must remain bent and your weight in your heels. The right hip bone (think of the right front pocket on your britches or pants) should come slightly further forward when you are imitating the right lead, and vice versa (figs. 6.9 A & B).

5. *Stand centered.* After cantering, step off the board and stand in a *normal riding position* on the ground (fig. 6.10). Bend your knees only slightly because your legs will be tired. The next step is perhaps the most important thing you'll learn from any exercise, so don't skip it. Close your eyes, and feel the great sense of balance and heaviness throughout your body. It should feel as if you've been on a boat, and you're now standing on solid ground for the first time in weeks. Other words to describe it include "planted," "stable," and "steady." You now feel something called *centered*, and this is exactly how you should feel when you're on

6.8 A–C Posting Trot

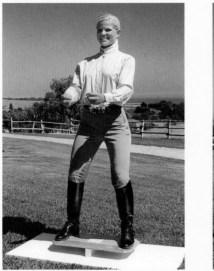

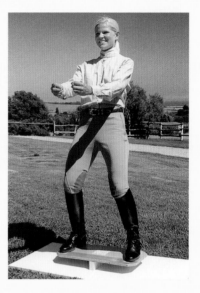

Stephanie is mimicking the posting trot by shifting her hips forward and backward while keeping her knees bent.

6.9 A & B The Canter

Stephanie's right hip comes forward while she imitates the right lead, and vice versa.

6.10 Centered Feeling

After completing your exercises, stand behind your board and close your eyes. You should feel balanced and stable.

your horse's back. Try to memorize this feeling and recapture it each time you ride. You can accomplish this by performing this 4-minute *Exercise One: The Riding Lesson*, as a regular warm-up just before mounting your horse.

EXERCISE TWO
The Jumping Test

This enjoyable exercise uses the walk, trot, and canter from *Exercise One: The Riding Lesson*, adding a few imaginary jumps to make it a little more challenging. Stand on your *Stable Board* and imagine you're a rider who's looking at a series of jumps of different heights and difficulties.

1. Assume your *normal riding position* and pick up the walk as you did in *Exercise One*. Imagine you are walking into an arena full of jumps of different sizes. Let this walk last about one minute.

2. After you've walked into the ring, pick up a sitting trot, and begin your imaginary warm-up by turning your horse in large circles, first to the left and then to the right. The important thing to

remember about circling is that your head, eyes, and shoulders should turn in the direction you are going, while your hips remain facing forward. If done correctly, your *Stable Board* will not rotate underneath you. If it does, your hips are either too stiff, or are following your shoulders through the turn instead of remaining forward. Do this for one minute (figs. 6.11 A & B).

3. Now, repeat your sitting trot turns while imitating the motion of the posting trot. You can even imagine shortening and lengthening your horse's stride by varying the amount of hip movement you use. Make these turns last for another full minute.

4. Now comes the interesting part. While standing on your board, pick up your canter (left lead to begin), and imagine that there is a small jump placed in front of you. Count to yourself, "Three, two, one, jump," and when you say the word "jump," actually leap up into the air for a split second and then land back on the board so that you're perfectly balanced with one foot on each stirrup (figs. 6.13 A – C). (See *Exercise Three* for more practice on jumping on the *Stable Board*).

5. As soon as you land, keep your eyes looking forward and canter toward your second imaginary fence. This one is a little bigger than the first, so you need to jump a little higher this time. As before, try landing so that you are perfectly balanced on your board. Once you get the hang of jumping, imagine that a jump is coming up on your left side. Look at it by turning your head, eyes, and shoulders in its direction, while keeping your hips facing forward. Now, imagine that this fence is directly in front of you, and jump it exactly as you did the first one. Your next jump will be on your right, so this time, you need to look right while keeping your hips facing forward. This isn't as easy as it sounds.

6. Once you get the hang of this exercise, "jump" a combination of two or three different jumps in a row, without looking down or taking the time to rebalance yourself.

7. After completing several jumps and jump combinations on both leads, stand on the ground, assume your *normal riding position*, close your eyes, and sense the same *centered* feeling you felt in the first exercise.

6.11 A & B Turning

When turning, you need to look in the direction of a turn without shifting your hips. Your shoulders should mirror the horse's shoulders and your hips mirror his hips.

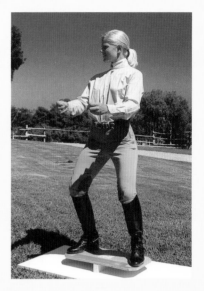

6.13 A–C Jumping

Stephanie jumps up and lands comfortably with her feet correctly back in the "stirrups."

The Jump for Joy exercise is described in detail below. Please note that although Stephanie is on her own in these photos, I recommend you do it with a partner holding your hands for safety.

Other Riding Disciplines

Even if you don't jump over fences in a ring, you can pretend to perform your very own riding discipline on the *Stable Board*. For instance, if you're a dressage rider, you can mimic the movements of 10 and 20 meter circles, and do flying changes of lead. If you're an event or trail rider, you can practice jumping your horse over small creeks and tree stumps while negotiating a twisty trail. Regardless of the type of riding you do, this short exercise can help you prepare for both the mental and physical challenges of your particular sport.

EXERCISE THREE
Jump for Joy—The Balance Test

This exercise improves awareness of your body and is designed to help you understand how your horse might feel if you ride unbalanced. Always use the *large, rectangular attachment.* You will need a partner for this exercise.

1. Begin by assuming your *normal riding position* with your right and left feet on the floor beside the right and left sides of your *Stable Board*. While in this starting position, look down at your board and make a mental note of where the two stirrups are. These are now your targets. (If you're using any other kind of balance board, you should draw a small target about 2 inches from each end.) The targets will tell you if you're jumping symmetrically or not. How they do will become clear in *Step Three*.

2. Lift your eyes so that you look straight forward (as if looking between your horse's ears), and resist the temptation to look down for the remainder of this step. Hold onto the hands of a friend, jump and land softly on the board so that both feet cover their targets. Immediately after landing, imitate the motion of the sitting trot without shifting the position of your feet, even if they don't feel accurately placed. It's very important that you don't look down or correct the position of your feet at this point.

3. Using only your body awareness for information, tell your partner how you landed. Is one foot closer to the center of the board? Is one foot toed-out or further forward than the

Landing positions

The position your feet land in while jumping on your board may be able to tell you a lot about the rest of your body.

1. If you consistently land with one foot pointed forward or slightly inward while the other is pointed outward, it likely indicates a hip stiffness on the side of your inward-facing foot.

2. If you land with one foot closer to the center of the board, it nearly always means that this inner leg and hip are stronger than the other leg.

3. If you land with one of your feet further forward on the board, it likely indicates a hip stiffness on this side of your body.

If you notice one or more of these three things while jumping on your board, you've probably also become aware that you consistently repeat them. It's important to realize that this is not just a coincidence, but a true indication of your body's symmetry.

Understanding this feedback has a positive effect on your mounted performance because it helps to diagnose faults with your actual riding. For instance, you may think you're giving equal right and left leg aids while riding, while you are unintentionally giving more of an aid with your stronger leg. When this occurs, your horse may misinterpret the leg aid you give for straightness as an aid for a lateral movement.

6.15 A – F Irregular Landing Positions

Photos A to C show commonly seen foot problems on landing—toeing out; one foot landing closer to the center; and one foot landing further forward. Photos D to F show Stephanie with more weight on one foot; looking down as she lands; and pinching with her knees.

other? Then, look down at your board, and see if your feet are where you thought. Don't be discouraged if, at first, your body awareness incorrectly estimates the location and position of your feet. Repeating this exercise will hone your awareness in no time. If you do land in a balanced position, the sitting trot will be easy to perform. (By the way, this effortless feeling is what your horse feels whenever you ride symmetrically, in good balance.) If you land with more weight on one foot, or with one foot closer to the center of the board, or with one foot further forward than the other, you'll find that the sitting trot—although possible—feels uncomfortable. This muscular tension and the torsion you feel in your body is what your horse must feel when you ride unbalanced (figs. 6.14 A–C).

4. After sitting the trot for 15 seconds, carefully step off the board and return to your starting position. Jump again, only this time, make adjustments for the faults you created and felt the first time. Continue doing this

exercise until you land in a perfectly balanced and symmetrical manner. Notice that when you land perfectly, you don't pull on your partner's hands for balance. This is exactly what happens when you ride for real—you are balanced and you don't pull on your horse's mouth.

EXERCISE FOUR
The Symmetry Slide

This exercise is the best symmetry-diagnostic tool of all. If there's any chance that one side of your body is stronger or more flexible than the other, this exercise will demonstrate it. To begin, place your *Stable Board* 6 inches away from a wall you can slide against (painted with enamel, for example), and assume your *normal riding position* with one foot on the ground beside each side of your board. Walls with a wood siding or covered with latex paint create friction, which inhibits your ability to smoothly slide up and down. Use the *small, round attachment*. You need a partner for this exercise (figs. 6.16 A–D).

1. In your starting position, place your hands on the wall behind you, and carefully lean back until your buttocks and back are pressing against it. Once comfortable, place your feet on the board so that they cover their stirrups. Hold your partner's hands during this portion of the exercise, and have her place her foot against the *Stable Board* so that it doesn't slip (see 6.5).

2. Standing comfortably on the board and leaning against the wall, assume your *normal riding position* and without looking down, shift the board so that it's flat from front-to-back and left-to-right. Once you think your board is flat, ask your partner to kneel down and check it, because even though you "feel" the board is perfectly balanced, it may not be so, and your body awareness is not as accurate as you expected. Then, ask your partner to put your body in a position so that the board is flat.

3. Place your hands together as if you are praying, and extend them well above your head. This lengthens your torso and makes it easier to see deficiencies in your balance and symmetry. When you're ready, carefully slide

6.16 A – D The Symmetry Slide

6.17 Have a Ball

Stephanie is demonstrating the starting position for this exercise. Note: as with The Symmetry Slide, you need a partner to help prevent the board slipping out from underneath you (as in 6.5).

Note that this exercise should be performed with a partner (as seen in 6.5). Stephanie is demonstrating without one for clarity of viewing, but it is not recommended. In photo A, she assumes the starting position with her hands on the wall for balance. In B, she is testing her awareness. She believes she has equal weight on both feet, even though she actually has a little more on her right foot. She starts to slide down well in C, but in D, you can see her body tightening causing her weight to shift to the right. She becomes asymmetrical.

down the wall by bending your knees. Pause for 5 seconds when you no longer feel comfortable, and slowly slide up the wall until you're in the starting position again.

4. Repeat this up-and-down motion until you feel your body moving in an even and symmetrical manner, and the board remains flat. Stop after 5 attempts and rest for a few minutes because this exercise can be a little stressful on your knees and muscles. If at any time you feel pain in your knees, back, or ankles, stop, and stretch the area for a few minutes. If this pain persists, stop altogether,

Play safe!

When performing *Stable Board* exercises, always follow these important safety tips.

1. Wear athletic shoes or paddock boots. Clogs and sandals are not recommended.

2. Avoid wearing socks only, because this may encourage you to try and hold onto the slick surface by gripping with your toes. The tension created in your feet will travel to your hips, knees, and lower back.

3. Work with a partner. When performing *Exercises Four* and *Five,* your partner should place one foot against the *Stable Board* to insure that it doesn't slip.

4. Don't place the *Stable Board* on a wet or dusty floor. These conditions may cause the board to slide unexpectedly.

5. Never close your eyes.

and move on to another exercise. (This exercise is not recommended for riders with knee and back problems.)

EXERCISE FIVE
Have a Ball

This exercise is similar to *The Symmetry Slide* with a few interesting changes. Instead of leaning back against a wall, you lean against a large, inflatable ball (see *Resources*, p. 168). To begin, place the ball up against a wall, assume your *normal riding position* while standing on the ground straddling your *Stable Board*, and lean into the ball so that it's pressing into the middle of your back just below your shoulder blades (fig. 6.17). Your legs must be spread wide enough so that your helper can place your *Stable Board* underneath you and between your feet. You can use the *large* or *small attachment* for this exercise.

1. Carefully, and with assistance (don't attempt this exercise alone), stand on the board so that your feet cover the targets, your weight is in your heels, and the ball remains pressed against the middle of your back.

2. Take a few seconds to balance yourself, and then slowly lower and raise your body a few inches by bending and extending your knees. You'll notice that this causes the ball to roll up and down your back, giving you a little back massage. Once you're comfortable with this up-and-down motion, refine it so that it mimics the actual motion and rhythm of the sitting trot. Sit the trot in this manner for one full minute, reminding yourself not to look down, hold your breath, pinch with your knees, or pull on your partner's hands for balance.

3. After you've completed the sitting trot, repeat the exercise exactly as in *Step One*, only this time, mimic the motion of the posting trot by pressing your buttocks toward the back wall and then letting them slowly rebound forward. The trick here is to always keep your weight in your heels. Continue to post to the trot in this manner for one minute, and then change your body's movement and rhythm so that it mimics the motion of the canter. You may find it particularly difficult to stay balanced while cantering on the right and left leads because you may feel that the ball is trying to force you off balance. Keep practicing, and you'll get used to it in no time.

PART THREE

FRAME AND FITNESS

THE TERM *RIDER FITNESS* DESCRIBES how the condition of your heart and lungs affects your ability to resist fatigue; the amount of strength, stamina, and flexibility possessed by your riding muscles; and the ability of your muscles, joints, ligaments, tendons, and bones to avoid or recover quickly from injury. The most important thing to remember about *rider fitness* is that no matter how fit your horse is, it'll be almost impossible for him to reach his full potential unless you're as fit as he is. Unfortunately, if you possess less-than-average fitness, you may not have the strength, stamina, flexibility, or control needed to overcome many of the obstacles that can come between you and effective riding. As I mentioned before, don't get fooled into thinking your horse is the only athlete in the arena. You, too, are an athlete, and your body has many important jobs to fulfill. You can teach it to perform these functions well by dedicating as much time and effort to your own fitness, as for your horse.

> ### It's all about you!
> Learn to improve the strength, stamina, and flexibility of your riding muscles, not so you can better control your horse, but so you can better control your own body while on your horse.

The Effects of Poor Rider Fitness

Remember the last time your instructor asked you to trot without stirrups? The words "drop your irons" may have caused you to consider riding right out of the ring and not stopping until you were safely hidden at home. The burn you feel when performing long-duration or complicated skills like no-stirrup work results from your muscles' inability to process enough fuel to continue working. This kind of fatigue can interfere with your desire to complete even a lesson itself. If you ever wish you could ride for longer without getting tired, you are wishing for better fitness and the "fatigue protection" that comes with it.

Being unfit can also cause many other rider problems:

1. Poor posture. As your body fatigues, the muscles of your torso (called your *upper-body stabilizers*) begin to run out of gas and cause you to slouch and round your shoulders, lean forward, or round your lower back. Since these flaws interfere with your balance and suppleness, you have to "hang-on" to your horse by squeezing with your already fatigued leg muscles. This creates a "vicious fitness circle" that can bring an early end to your lesson—and perhaps even a few riding dreams.

2. Decreased mental capacities. As you tire, your muscles become starved of oxygen and are forced to look elsewhere for this important fuel. Often, they find it on its way to your brain and steal some of it away. Mental capacity including your coordination, concentration, mental focus, reflexes, reactions, and other decision-making processes are ultimately harmed. Increasing the efficiency with which your muscles use their own supply of oxygen is the only way to avoid this problem.

"Get off my back... please!"

Around the same time that your body starts showing signs of fatigue, your horse will also be feeling a little tired. While giving in to the fatigue (by leaning forward and rounding your shoulders) may help you save energy, it makes your horse do more work. The next time you feel tired in the saddle, remind yourself that you're an athlete, sit up straight, take in a deep breath, and push yourself a little harder so that your horse doesn't have to work extra hard to carry your tired body around.

3. Poor biomechanics. Even if you're normally blessed with good symmetry, balance, breathing, and body awareness, poor fitness can cause these attributes to weaken quickly. The postural flaws and muscle fatigue related to poor fitness are usually to blame.

4. Increased risk of injury. When your muscles tire and your posture, mental capacity, rider-aids, balance, and symmetry are compromised, the possibility of suffering a riding-related mishap increases. While falling causes some injuries, many others such as lower back pain, knee discomfort, and pulled muscles are caused by poorly prepared muscles. When your fitness improves, so do your chances of avoiding riding injuries.

5. Weakened natural aids. As your body begins to feel the effects of fatigue, your muscles lose much of their control and dexterity. Your ability to deliver precise and timely aids decreases, as does your ability to com-municate with your horse. The following demonstrates the results of riding fit and riding unfit.

Different kinds of discomfort zones

Hunched forward: When the core muscles of your back and stomach get tired, your body tries to conserve energy by rounding your shoulders and back. Imagine the stance of a runner hunched over with his hands on his knees after completing a grueling race (A).

Have-a-seat: This is when you try to ease the burn in your muscles by leaning back and sitting in an imaginary, chair instead of holding yourself erect and transferring your weight into your heels.

Unfortunately, this places all of your weight on your horse's spine and kidney area, something that obviously causes him discomfort (B).

Sack of potatoes: When you just can't go on, all your muscles give up at the same time, and your once attractive conformation now looks more like a heavy bag of potatoes (C).

Asymmetrical: For a description, see *Your Discomfort Zone,* p. 67. Both the rider and I are showing this tendency (D).

7.1 A–D Discomfort Zones

Your Discomfort Zone

No matter how much you've improved your balance and symmetry, you risk returning to your old, bad asymmetrical habits whenever your muscles become fatigued in the saddle. Imagine having to stand in one place for two hours without moving. In the beginning you feel fine, but as your muscles begin to tire you probably drop a shoulder, shift your hips to one side, place more weight in the leg on that side, and round your shoulders forward. If you're unfit, there's a good chance you'll also achieve this very same asymmetrical stance while in the saddle. I call this the *discomfort zone*, because while it may seem comfortable to you, it causes your horse a good deal of discomfort.

Poor Fitness and Its Effect on a Rider's Aids

- You're physically fatigued when you ask your horse to perform a movement.

- Your tired muscles weaken your dexterity and body control so your horse can't understand the aids.

- You reapply the aids in the hope your horse reads your mind, but he responds incorrectly and becomes tense and confused.

- You're frustrated but reapply the aids again, and out of the goodness of his heart, he responds the way you wanted.

- Your body continues to deliver unintentional and confusing aids causing your horse to become more tense and harder to manage.

- Fatigue and frustration finally get the best of you. You dismount and blame your horse for everything that's wrong with the world.

Good Fitness and Its Effect on a Rider's Aids

- You feel fresh so you ask your horse to perform a movement by applying the aids in a precise and timely manner.

- Your horse clearly understands the request and performs it quickly and correctly.

- You reward your horse with a pat on the neck, and he continues to perform the movement correctly.

- You still feel fresh so you ask for another movement by applying a different set of precise and timely aids.

- Your horse understands, quickly picks up the new task, and appreciates the manner in which you're riding.

The Blue Ribbon List

Improved fitness helps you to *Ride Right*. I call the many advantages gained *The Blue Ribbon List*.

Build strong and fatigue-resistant riding muscles.
Lower the risk and seriousness of riding injuries.
Undo the effects of age and previous injuries.
Enhance your body awareness, reactions, and reflexes.

Refine your sense of balance and breathing.
Improve your mounted posture and symmetry.
Boost your energy, mental ability, and confidence.
Build supple and flexible muscles, tendons, and ligaments.
Optimize your leg, seat, body, and rein aids.
Neutralize the effect that poor-rider fitness has on your horse.

How Much is Enough?

To determine how often you must exercise to achieve "Blue Ribbon" results, you need to take into consideration your current level of fitness, body type, and something called your *activity level*. There are four different levels of activity: *sedentary*, *moderate*, *active*, and *intense*. In order to maintain or improve your current level of fitness, you must remain at least *moderately active*.

1. Sedentary. Most riders don't fall into this category because riding is a physically active sport. If you're sedentary now but want to improve your fitness, start out slowly to avoid injury. You wouldn't jump into the deep end of a pool if you didn't already know how to swim so don't make the same mistake with your fitness.

2. *Moderate*. You're moderately active if you ride or exercise two or three times a week. Congratulations for making the effort, but try to find a few sneaky ways to increase your activity to the next level. An early morning trail ride or doing a few rider-specific exercises from this book will do the trick. Use your imagination to find a few fun and easy ways to increase your activity level.

3. *Active*. You're active if you ride or exercise at least 4 to 6 times a week. If this describes you, keep up the good work and continue to feel great and ride wonderfully. You can avoid feeling burnt-out by varying your program regularly—something you can do by simply adding a few new unmounted exercises to your current riding program.

4. *Intense*. This category describes you if rotten little things like work interfere with your program of riding or exercising several times a day. Ensure that your body remains healthy by including at least one day of rest and two days of light activity each week, as over-training can be just as harmful as under-training.

CHAPTER EIGHT

STRENGTH

In riding, strength is a confusing issue because it is usually considered a good attribute. However, for riders *too much* muscle mass interferes with flexibility, and *too little* makes it difficult to perform many important riding tasks. The key to achieving the perfect amount of strength is to develop sinewy, supple, and moderately strong muscles (by performing exercises using very light weights and doing lots of repetition. When you develop the correct kind of strength and muscle, you'll have the force needed to impart effective aids and maintain a good posture, as well as the flexibility needed to ride in a supple manner.

Muscular strength is defined as *the maxi-mum amount of force a muscle can exert*. While this definition is suitable for most sports, it lacks a few important details when it comes to riding. Athletes such as football players can use this definition because their job is to make one single hit with as much force as possible. Immediately afterward, they return to the huddle to rest up for the next maximum hit (and look for any missing teeth).

Strength while riding is different because you need to use your muscles as economically as possible so that you can continue riding without resting. Applying one maximum leg aid to ask for a simple trot transition, for instance, will not only lead to exhaustion, it'll

The dynamic duo

You've likely noticed when riding that some of your muscles move a lot while others don't move at all. So why is it that they all seem to get tired?

- Muscles contract two ways: *dynamic* or *static.* Regardless of which way they contract, they are always subject to fatigue.

- *Dynamic* muscle contractions are called *isotonic* and always result in some visible movement of your body or one of its parts. Opening and closing your hip angle while posting the trot is a good example of a *dynamic* contraction. Disciplines such as polo and roping employ this kind of strength.

- *Static* muscle contractions are called *isometric* and never result in visible motion of your body or any of its parts. The strength that your back, shoulders, and abdominal muscles expend to control your posture is a good example of an isometric contraction. Even though there's no visible movement, they're still working very hard. When they begin to get tired, they weaken and that is when some movement occurs. Shoulders that sag and a back that begins to round are two good examples.

- *Dynamic* and *static* muscle contractions are the *Dynamic Duo*, the "Batman and Robin," of muscle control, working together to make your muscles move in the most effective and efficient way possible.

The rider's strength-training dictionary

If you don't know weights from waffles, you should familiarize yourself with a few important strength-training terms. Once you become more acquainted with these terms, you'll have an easier time understanding the exercises at the end of this chapter.

Effort

The actual movement you do to complete a motion. At times, you may lift, pull, push, or even squeeze, but regardless of the motion, it will always be called an *effort*.

Repetition

The number of times you can complete an effort. If you do 12 rider-specific sit-ups, you've completed 12 repetitions.

Sets

The number of times you're able to complete your repetitions. If you do 12 rider-specific sit-ups, take a rest, then do 12 more, you've completed 2 sets of 12.

A heavy weight

A weight that's so heavy you can only lift it 8 times before having to sacrifice good form. Heavy weights are associated with stiff muscles and poor flexibility, so avoid lifting them.

A medium weight

A challenging weight that you can lift 9 to 20 times without sacrificing good form.

A light weight

The best kind of weight because it helps you develop strong, yet supple, and fatigue-resistant muscles. This weight is light enough so that you can lift it repeatedly for a long period of time without sacrificing good form.

Contraction

The phase of the *effort* when your muscle is working. The mechanism behind a contraction is a shortening of your muscle and its fibers. When you do a rider-specific sit-up, for instance, this is the phase when your abdominal muscles contract, thereby causing you to "sit up." Remember that a contraction can either cause a part of your body to move *(dynamic)* or cause no movement whatsoever *(static)*.

Elongation

The phase of the *effort* when your muscle is at rest. The mechanism behind an elongation is a relaxation or lengthening of your muscle and its fibers. When you do a rider-specific sit-up, this is the phase when you relax your stomach muscles, and your body lowers itself to the ground.

also cause your horse to become very cranky. You might as well put on a helmet and join the football players in the huddle. Remember that the way you use your strength is just as important as the amount of strength you use. When you learn to use your strength in an economical and effective manner, you'll never have to worry about your horse using his maximum force against you.

Another difference between riders and other athletes is the way in which your muscles perform their jobs. Instead of delivering fast or powerful movements like smashing a tennis ball or hitting a hockey puck, you usually only use your muscles to perform small subtle movements. When you use your muscles like this, you're able to quickly adjust to the actions of your horse and keep him moving in a balanced and effective way. Applying light pressure with your left hand, then the right, and then left again to keep your horse's mouth supple and "on the bit," is a good example of subtle strength.

The Strength-Training Rules

Abiding by the following seven rules will help you protect your body against injury and increase your strength without sacrificing your flexibility. Since strength training places an unfamiliar amount of stress on your body, it's important that you perform your exercises in the safest way possible.

1. Always warm up and stretch. In order to avoid injuries that can bring your good intentions to a premature halt, always prepare your muscles, tendons, and ligaments for the stress that's about to come. Four or 5 minutes of the warm-up exercises and stretches in this book can help you achieve this (p. 102).

2. Lift the proper amount. Large, bulky muscles interfere with your flexibility and harm your riding, so to ensure that the muscles you build are supple, lift light weights only. Remember that these are the weights you can lift repeatedly for a long period of time without sacrificing your good form.

3. Exercise in your "normal riding position." Regardless of the exercise, always perform it so that your body imitates your actual riding. Extend your arms in front of your body as if holding a pair of reins, bend and open your knees, look forward, and open your shoulders. This imitation will ensure the exercise benefits transfer to your mounted performance. Pay special attention to your symmetry, balance, breathing, and body awareness.

4. Do each repetition slowly and smoothly. If you race through an exercise, you'll use more momentum than muscle and cheat your body out of the exercise benefits. Make the contraction phase of each effort last 3 seconds and the elongation phase last about four. When you increase the speed, you decrease the benefits.

5. No bouncing. Allowing your muscles to bounce between the contraction and elongation phase can lead to injury. As if this isn't bad enough, a mechanism called the *stretch reflex* will kick in and do most of the work for your muscles. Once again, your body will be robbed of its deserved benefits. Avoid this by pausing for at least 1 full second between the contraction and elongation phases of each repetition.

6. Perform isometric and isotonic contractions. To ride effectively, you must constantly perform both *dynamic* and *static* movements. While most exercise programs only include *dynamic* movements, your program should include both. Get the most out of your exercises by varying the duration and frequency of your *dynamic* movements and *static* holds. For instance, start with 5 *dynamic* movements followed by a 5-second *static* hold, and then do 10 *dynamic* movements followed by a 10-second *static* hold (see Sidebar, p. 69).

7. Don't overdo it. Even if you're anxious to see results right away, overdoing it isn't going to get you there any faster. In fact, exercising in an overzealous manner will likely slow your progress because it causes your muscle fibers to break down, often leading to weakness, pain, and injury. Start out by limiting your strength-training sessions to a maximum of 3 times a week. Once your body is accustomed to the stress of the exercises, increase the frequency to 4 or even 5 times a week. Regardless of how many times you exercise, it's important that you never work the same muscle two days in a row. You must give muscles the rest they need by allowing them a full 48 hours before working them again. During this rest period, your body will heal all your muscle micro-tears, a process that eventually leaves them stronger than before. For more information about protecting your muscles against injury, read Chapter Twelve, but for now, it's sufficient to say that more is not always better when it comes to strength training.

Your Riding Muscles

Over 40 percent of a man's body and 30 percent of a woman's is made up of muscle. Riding uses almost every muscle in your body, and it's not unusual for you to use as many as 10 or 15 different ones to achieve a simple movement. While some muscles work to control your posture, and some make it possible to apply leg aids, others open and close your hips. Of all your muscles, those that are most important are the ones that make up your legs, hips, back, buttocks, shoulders, and abdominals (fig. 8.1). When used properly, these muscles help you develop good posture, balance, symmetry, rhythm, aids, and shock absorption, and work together to help you control your body so that your horse can control his. The following is a list of the most important riding muscles and the jobs they perform:

1. *Back muscles (latissimus dorsi, erector spinae, spinalis, and longissimus)* control the torsion and twisting motion of your upper body, open your shoulders, and help you maintain a proper and erect posture.

2. *Shoulder muscles (trapezius, deltoids, rhomboids major and minor, and triceps)* are responsible for opening your shoulders and upper arms. They also play an important role in posture and make it possible for you to apply precise rein aids while allowing your arms to follow the motion of your horse's mouth.

3. *Abdominal muscles (rectus abdominis, internal obliques, external obliques, and transverse abdominis)* are important because they stabilize your torso, prevent excessive curvature of your lower back, and control the twisting motion of your body while turning. They also help control the rhythmic motion of your hips and make possible movements that require a pelvic tilt, such as the deep-seated canter and the half-halt.

4. *Hip muscles (iliopsoas, iliacus, and the psoas major and minor)* flex and extend your hips, making movements such as the canter and posting trot possible. It's important that these muscles remain both strong and supple.

5. *Buttock muscles (gluteus maximus, medius, and minimus)* stabilize your pelvis, spread your hips and knees, and provide impulsion and power while riding. They also work with your abdominal muscles to help you achieve a deep seat and pelvic tilt.

6. *Quadriceps (quadriceps femoris, rectus emoris, and the vastus lateralis, intermedius, and medius)* are responsible for flexing your hips, extending your knees, and allowing you to achieve the long-leg position necessary for motions such as the two-point position, post-

ing trot, canter, and jumping.

7. *Hamstrings (semimembranosus, semitendinosus, and biceps femoris)* help you apply leg aids by extending your hip joints and flexing your knees and allow you to achieve a deep seat by tilting your pelvis slightly backward. When your hamstrings are tight, your lower back is forced to round. Supple hamstrings, therefore, also play a major role in good posture.

8. *Hip rotators (sartorius, piriformis, and obturator externus)* make it possible for you to rotate or pivot your upper and lower legs so that they can more easily lie against the barrel-shaped body of your horse. This action is also what makes the toes-out position and the application of lateral aids possible. When a rider pinches with her knees, she's usually contracting these muscles along with those of the following group.

9. *Adductors (pectineus, gracilis, and the adductor brevis, longus, and magnus)* are located on the inside of your thighs and work together as a group to help your legs maintain contact with your horse and apply lateral aids. If you "grip" too tightly with these muscles (hang on with your legs), the muscular tension created by them can have a negative effect on the flexibility of the other muscles in your thigh area, particularly your hips. It's also not

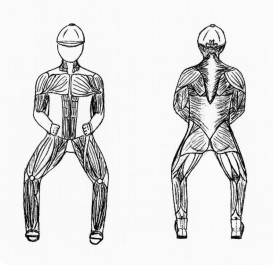

8.1 Muscles Used in Riding

uncommon for you to squeeze your body slightly upward. This has a negative effect on your balance because it narrows your base of support and raises your center of balance.

10. *The muscles of your shin areas (tibialis anterior)* perform two important jobs. Their main job is called *dorsiflexion*, an action that allows you to lower your heels into the "heels-down" position, and their second job is called *inversion*, an action that allows your lower legs to contact your horse's sides while your feet are facing forward. Dressage riders use these muscles every time they apply leg aids with the insides of their lower legs.

Five Strength-Enhancing Exercises

As mentioned earlier, rider-specific exercise must imitate and exaggerate the most challenging movements of the horse and rider; target your riding muscles; be safe, enjoyable, and convenient; and be performed in such a way that won't jeopardize your health. To accomplish this, you should start by doing only 1 or 2 sets of each exercise. Once your body becomes stronger and more resistant to fatigue, you can increase the workload to as many as 3 or 4 sets of each exercise. If you haven't taken the time to read *The Strength-Training Dictionary* and *Rules* as outlined on pages 70–1, do so before attempting any of the following five exercises.

EXERCISE ONE
Sitting Around

Sitting Around, which is very similar to the strength test (see Sidebar, *Test Your Static Muscle Strength*, p. 74), does a great job of improving the *static* strength of your hips, quadriceps, hamstrings, buttocks, and shin muscles. You'll need a *Stable Board,* a helper, and a clean wall area. You can use either the *large* or *small board attachment.*

1. Place the *Stable Board* about 8 inches from the wall. With your partner close by, place your buttocks and hands firmly against the wall. Slide down the wall until your thighs are extended slightly out in front of you and your left foot is on the floor beside the left side of your *Stable Board*, and your right foot

> ## "Your hip bone's connected to your thigh bone..."
> A weakness in one muscle will compromise the integrity of the muscles surrounding it. This well-known children's song does a good job of explaining this. For instance, when your hip muscles are weak, there's a good chance your knee and inner-thigh muscles will be weak as well. This is why it's so important to strengthen each and every one of your riding muscles. The exercises in this chapter can help you do this.

is on the floor beside the right side of your board.

2. Holding your partner's hands, place your feet on the *Stable Board* so that each foot covers its stirrup. Without letting go of your partner's hands, carefully slide your body down the wall further, until your knees are bent at more than a 45-degree angle, but less than 90 degrees (figs. 8.2 A & B). You should feel the front part of your thighs begin to burn almost immediately. It's crucial that you don't let go of your partner's hands and also important that he places his foot against the *Stable Board* to prevent it from slipping.

3. *Statically* hold this position for 45 seconds or as long as you can. Continue to hold your partner's hands as if they were a pair of reins, open your knees, and breathe rhythmically. You may feel a slight muscular contraction on the outside part of your hips and buttocks as you do this.

4. During the 45-second *static* hold, repeatedly lift your toes off the board. This constant up-and-down motion will cause your shin muscles to burn and your weight to stay in your heels.

5. After the full 45 seconds, have your partner pull you up to the original standing posi-

tion on the board. Slowly, step off the board with the assistance of your partner. Repeat this exercise a second time before moving on.

When performing *Sitting Around*, the muscles of your *lower* body will fatigue and burn. This is normal, but the muscles of your *upper* body should not become tense as well. You should also not hold your breath when you perform a *static* contraction. To avoid these problems, make an effort to keep your upper body supple and relaxed, and breathe easily and rhythmically. The ability to do this will give you increased confidence in the future when exposed to riding situations that require your upper and lower body to work independently of one another. Lastly, focus your eyes forward, and keep your knees open during the entire exercise.

EXERCISE TWO
Lunge Time

Lunge Time does a very good job of improving your balance, symmetry, and body awareness, while strengthening the muscles of your hamstrings, quadriceps, buttocks, and hips. What I like most about this exercise is that it forces you to listen to your body as well as your partner's, something you must always do when working with your horse. If you aren't able to understand your partner's body language, you're going to have a difficult time completing the exercise.

1. Begin by facing your partner, and place your *Stable Board* on the floor between you. Use the *large board attachment* at first, and change it to the *smaller, round board attachment* as soon as you get the hang of this exercise.

2. Holding onto your partner's hands for balance and safety, carefully place your left foot on the board so that it covers the stirrup. Your right foot should remain on the ground well behind the center of the *Stable Board*. Once you're comfortably balanced in this position, have your helper place his left foot on the stirrup. Both of you should now have your left feet on the board and your right feet on the ground (fig. 8.3 A).

3. Here comes the hard part: working together (as you must do with your horse), balance the board without looking down. To do this, you must become aware of your body as well as your partner's. Bend your knees, relax, and focus your eyes forward.

4. Once the board is balanced, start moving your bodies—bending and extending your knees—so that they imitate the motion of the sitting trot. If done correctly, both bodies will move together (*dynamic muscle contractions*) in an up-and-down motion with similar rhythm and cadence, and the *Stable Board* will remain still. Continue to hold hands for 15 seconds and remember not to look down.

5. After 15 seconds, you should be feeling

more balanced and secure, so change your full-handed grip to index fingers only. Continue the "sitting trot" in this manner for another 15 seconds. Then completely release hands (unless you're feeling unbalanced, in which case you should continue to hold with index fingers), and do the "sitting trot" for a final 15 seconds with your hands held forward as if holding a pair of imaginary reins (figs. 8.3 B & C).

6. While holding your imaginary reins, stop the sitting-trot motion, and change to a motion that mimics the movement of the posting trot. Continue "posting to the trot" in this manner for a full 45 seconds. Even if your lower body is starting to burn, make an effort to keep your upper body, arms, and hands soft and supple.

7. Finish the exercise by changing your body's motion to the canter (you'll notice you're "cantering" on the left lead because your left hip is slightly in front of your right). Continue to "canter" on the left lead for 45 seconds.

8. Before stepping off your board, stop your *dynamic* canter motion altogether, and remain still (*static muscle contractions*) for 15 seconds. You can now end the exercise by grasping hands again and helping each other off the board. Rest for 60 seconds, and then repeat the exercise with your other leg. When you've finished working both sides, you'll have exercised your entire lower body in both a *dynamic* and *static* manner.

EXERCISE THREE
Symmetry Stomach

I designed *Symmetry Stomach* to improve the strength of your stomach, lower back, and hip muscles. Visit any gym today, and you'll see a dozen different people doing a dozen different abdominal exercises or versions of sit-ups. While normal sit-ups are a good way to

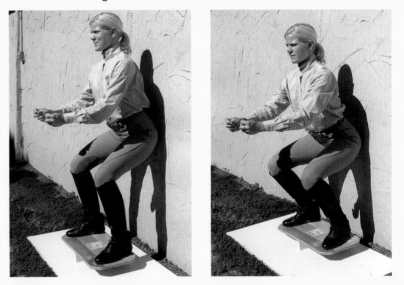

8.2 A & B Sitting Around

In A, the basic sitting-around position is shown. (Note: when you do this, I recommend that you hold a partner's hands as if they were a pair of reins, and have the partner brace the Stable Board for safety as in 6.5). In B, Stephanie is sitting down too far—her knees are out further than her toes.

improve the strength of your lower torso, the majority of them don't have all the ingredients necessary to improve your riding. So, I've developed the rider's sit-up, which doesn't just improve the muscle strength in your back, hips, and stomach, it also helps refine your sense of balance, symmetry, and body awareness.

1. Place your *Stable Board* on the floor in an uncluttered area. Start this exercise with the *large attachment*, but swap it for the more difficult, *smaller attachment* once you've become proficient. Carefully place your hands on the floor behind the board and lower yourself to a sitting position on the board so that your seat bones are an equal distance from the center. *Do not* wrap your fingers around the sides of board (fig. 8.4 A).

2. Once you feel comfortable in the sitting position, lean backward a few inches and place the majority of your body weight in your hands on the ground. You'll now be sitting on your back pockets and have a very good feel of each seat bone on the board. Do

This exercise strengthens the hamstrings, quadriceps, buttocks, and hip muscles. Photo A shows the starting position, and B and C demonstrate how the riders move their bodies by bending and extending their knees to imitate the motion of the sitting trot.

you have the same amount of weight in each one? You can place a medium-sized gym ball between your calves (not your knees, as this will teach you to pinch with them) to make the exercise a little more challenging (see *Resources*, p. 168).

3. Once you're balanced in this position, lift your feet off the ground, open your knees, and place your feet in a heels-down position. Pause a few seconds to regain your balance, and then do a slow *dynamic* contraction of your stomach and hip muscles so that your knees come toward your chest and your chest comes toward your knees in an accordion-type fashion (figs. 8.4 B–D). Pause again for one second (*static* muscle contraction), and then slowly lower your chest and knees to their starting position without letting your feet touch the ground. At this point, you can still use your hands to help maintain your balance. Do 15 repetitions before stopping.

4. After you've completed 15 repetitions, take a short rest while remaining seated on your board. Repeat the sit-ups as before, only

this time, make your *dynamic* and *static* muscle contractions much quicker and smaller so that your body imitates the movement of the sitting trot. Sit the trot in this manner for 30 seconds or until you can no longer continue comfortably.

5. Take another rest. Then repeat *Step Four* exactly as above, only this time try to do it without placing your hands on the floor behind you. You may want to start by using just three fingers, then only index fingers, followed by thumbs for balance. Once you're comfortable without your hands, place your arms in front of your body as if holding a pair of reins. Obviously, this is going to be much more difficult, but keep trying, and in no time, you'll be able to "sit the trot" for 30 seconds without using your hands for balance.

6. Before finishing, perform one last dynamic contraction of your stomach muscles by bringing your knees toward your chest. Once there, hold them in a static position for 10 seconds. Slowly, lower them back to their starting position, and statically hold them

there for another 10 seconds. You've just exercised your entire lower torso in both a dynamic and static way.

EXERCISE FOUR
The Big Squeeze

I designed *The Big Squeeze* to improve your inner thigh strength while also improving your balance, symmetry, and body awareness. If you visit your local gym, you'll likely find a few machines that improve your inner thigh strength, but the majority of these make you to do the exercises in a seated position. While this ensures comfort, it unfortunately also means that you receive little or no balance, symmetry, or body-awareness benefit. So, do *The Big Squeeze* in a standing position, together with a partner to help with balance. The partner is closely involved and benefits from this exercise, too. If you'd like to do this exercise but don't have a partner, place one end of the rubber exercise band (see next paragraph) around your leg and the other end around a low, fixed object, such as a fence post.

1. Begin by standing beside your partner, and put a rubber, exercise band (available in all sporting goods stores) around your right ankle. Now, place the band around your partner's left ankle. (When purchasing such a band, ask for one that has light-to-medium resistance, because a band with heavy resistance can cause you to sacrifice your *normal riding position* during the exercise. See *Resources,* p. 168.)

2. Once the band is secured, take one step sideways away from each other while inter-

8.4 A–D The Symmetry Stomach

Photo A shows the starting position; In B to D, Stephanie is doing slow, dynamic contractions of her muscles so that her knees go back-and-forth from her chest in an accordian-like fashion.

This exercise improves inner thigh strength. After applying the rubber exercise band around both your ankles, start with your arms interlocking as in A, and perform the exercises as described in the text and demonstrated in B and C. Note that in these last two pictures the riders are performing the exercise with their hands in the rein-holding position. This is more difficult and requires your close attention, not only to your own balance and breathing, but also your partner's.

locking arms for balance. Both of you should pause briefly, then slowly bend your knees, shift your body weight to your outside leg (the one without the band), lift your inside leg off the floor, and place your elevated foot in the heels-down position. Now, you'll both be balanced on your outside leg (fig. 8.5 A).

3. Both of you should pause briefly again to regain your balance, and slowly contract your inner thigh muscles. When done correctly, your inside leg will move slowly toward your outside leg, in much the same way as your leg moves when delivering an actual leg aid. When your legs touch, squeeze your inner thigh muscles hard in an inward and slightly upward manner for 5 seconds (fig. 8.5 B). Your inside leg will now be *statically* pressing into your outside ankle. While performing this leg aid, imagine that you're giving a lateral aid to your horse while trying to lift his body and round his back.

4. After the 5 second *static* hold, both of you should slowly relax your inner thigh muscles so that your inside legs slowly return to their original position. Once there, don't allow your inside feet to touch the ground, and repeat the in-and-out motion again 9 more times without losing your balance (fig. 8.5 C).

5. Once you've finished the 10 repetitions, take a short break, and repeat the exercise exactly as before, only this time without holding onto your partner's arm for balance—but still connected by the exercise band. This is going to be a lot harder. Pay very close attention to your balance and breathing, and remain acutely aware of your partner's body and movements as they can still have a big influence on your rhythm and balance. After finishing this exercise with one leg, change the bands around, and repeat it on the opposite side.

8.6 A–D The Rein Aid

In photos A to C, in the normal riding position, the rider demonstrates the back-and-forth motion that strengthens the upper-body muscles. In D, she is in the two-point riding position.

EXERCISE FIVE
The Rein Aid

The final strength-training exercise, *The Rein Aid*, focuses on the important muscles of your upper body. Since they're responsible for everything from steering to braking, you should make an effort to improve their performance, as well. As in *Exercise Four*, this uses a rubber, exercise band. Since your arms are naturally weaker than your thighs, use only a light-resistance band (see *Resources*, p. 168).

1. Start by placing the band around a vertical portion of a swinging gate or the doorknob of an open door (fig. 8.6 A). The gate or open door can give you some very important clues about your upper body symmetry. I'll tell you more about this in *Step Four*.

2. With the band placed around the gate or doorknob, hold onto its ends as if they're a pair of reins, and assume your *normal riding position*.

3. Slowly pull back on the band without shifting your weight forward or backward. Pay special attention to your shoulders because you don't want them moving backward or forward. Simply use your upper back and triceps muscles to cause this exaggerated reining action—without the help of the rest of your body. Do this by trying to touch your shoulder blades together (fig. 8.6 B).

4. Once you've pulled your arms back as far as possible, hold them *statically* for 5 seconds (don't forget to breathe), and then slowly relax your arms and let the band return to

its starting position (fig. 8.6 C). You should not feel your weight shift from your heels to your toes during this motion, and the door should not swing in one direction or the other. If it swings to the left, you are pulling more with your left arm, and if it swings to the right, you're pulling more with your right.

Keep the door from swinging, and you'll learn how to use equal rein tension.

5. Repeat this pulling-and-holding motion 10 times.

6. You can also perform this exercise standing in the *two-point riding position* (fig. 8.6 D).

※

CHAPTER NINE

STAMINA

The term *rider stamina* is used to describe the way in which your body resists and tolerates the physical fatigue of riding. When your resistance is high, you can ride in an effective manner for what seems like forever. As soon as your tolerance drops, however, your riding ability drops as well. If, for instance, your back muscles succumb to muscular fatigue, you'll have a difficult time maintaining a proper posture, giving effective body and seat aids, and keeping your hips supple and tension-free.

Without stamina, you'll likely end up exhausted on your horse's back in a "swimming pool" of sweat. Since this isn't exactly the kind of swimming you normally associate with athletes and endurance, you should do all you can to avoid it. Regardless of whether you're a weekend rider or an Olympic competitor, you, your horse, and your riding performance will all benefit from improved endurance.

Your body relies on three different kinds of *stamina*: *muscular*, *cardiovascular*, and *psychological*. The good news is that an increase in one type of *stamina* nearly always causes an increase in the others. The not-so-good news is that in order for you to increase your *stamina,* you're going to have to do a little hard work.

In this chapter, I will explain five different methods of stamina-improving training, some ways to vary these methods to maximize the physical benefits, specific exercises for each method, various tests to help provide you with an idea of what kind of shape you are in, and what kind of work you need to do in order to reach your stamina goals. Most importantly, the information is all rider-specific, so you'll never be far, albeit conceptually at times, from the back of your horse.

Muscular Stamina

Muscular stamina is your ability to exert a muscular contraction and sustain it over a long period of time. This type of stamina dictates how long you can exert a *dynamic* effort like the posting trot, or a *static* effort like maintaining good posture before fatigue or *muscle burn* brings the effort to a halt.

The longer you can delay the burn, the longer you can ride with good form and function. There are three ways to improve your muscular stamina, *long-duration riding, aerobic exercise,* and *repetitive strength training* with light weights. No matter how much time you've spent on improving your symmetry and balance, your body will return to its old, bad habits if you don't have enough muscular stamina. Think back to the part in this book on your *discomfort zone* where I asked you to imagine standing still for a long period of time without moving (p. 67). If you're like most riders, you can probably stand straight for a while, but as soon as your muscular stamina goes away, you'll assume your discomfort zone by shifting your hips to one side, placing more weight in one leg, and rounding your shoulders forward. This compromise is not caused by poor symmetry or posture, but by poor muscular stamina.

Cardiovascular Stamina

Cardiovascular stamina is your heart's and lungs' ability to supply your hard-working muscles with oxygen during vigorous activities. If you quickly become out of breath while exercising or riding, your body cannot

> *You perform a triathlon every time you ride. Instead of swimming, biking, and running, you walk, trot, and canter!*

resist fatigue or recover quickly from it. Since a lack of cardiovascular stamina, just like a lack of muscular stamina, can bring your good riding intentions to an abrupt halt, you should always make an effort to keep your heart and lungs in good physical shape.

To achieve this, you need to physically push your body past the point it's normally accustomed to going. This is called *progressive overload*, and although it requires hard work on your part, the riding improvements you'll be rewarded with make it well worth your while.

Psychological Stamina

The third kind of stamina, *psychological stamina*, refers to your ability to remain mentally focused on a riding task, even though your body is physically fatigued. Swift, precise, and appropriate decisions are important in order to keep your horse moving in a proper frame and attitude, so you should always ensure that your mental capacities are functioning well. To do this, you need your brain to receive as much fuel—delivered in the form of oxygen-rich blood—as possible. Without this fuel, many of your cognitive skills including reflex, reaction, timing, judgment, and body awareness will suffer. Make sure your oxygen-delivery system is always working at optimum performance.

Improve Your Stamina

There are several different methods of increasing *muscular*, *cardiovascular*, and *psychological stamina*. All methods achieve their goal by encouraging you to physically push yourself past the exertion level you're normally accustomed to—that is, *progressive overload*. This overload does not need to be excessive, however. It can simply mean taking a brisk walk if you're sedentary, or going for a slow jog if you only normally take walks. Exercising using the overload principle is linked to numerous fitness benefits, including a delay in the onset of lactic acid production in your muscles, greater mental strength and confidence in your ability to continue on, and an improved ability of your heart and lungs to deliver oxygen-rich blood to your muscles and brain. Theses are the kinds of physical and mental benefits that can help you in your quest to *Ride Right*. There are five common, and very effective, stamina-enhancing methods that utilize the theory behind the overload principle listed below. (Starting on page 90, I give you specific exercises for these methods.)

1. Circuit Training. This kind of program improves your stamina because it encourages you to perform several strength-training exercises at different exercise "stations," one after another, in an aerobic manner. All the exercises are different and are performed next to each other to minimize travel and rest time between each exercise station. You rapidly perform a strength-enhancing exercise with a very light weight for a specific amount of time (usually 45 to 60 seconds), then rest while walking over to the next exercise (about 15 seconds). Once you arrive, you perform the new exercise for the same amount of time as the first. You continue to perform your rider-specific exercises in this aerobic manner, until you've completed all of them, usually about 5 to 15 different ones. Once you've completed one full "circuit" of all the exercises, start again and complete it a second, or even a third time. *Circuit Training* not only improves your stamina, it's a great way to avoid exercise boredom. (See *The Balance Ball*, p. 90.)

2. *Cross-Training*. Just like *Circuit Training*, the purpose of *Cross-Training* is to improve your stamina while helping you avoid boredom and burnout. It's also very effective at giving your hardest working muscles a rest while you continue to improve your overall stamina. *Cross-Training* accomplishes this by encouraging you to mix up the unmounted exercises you perform. Instead of performing the same exercise day after day, you add a variety of other exercises or activities to your program. If you ride every Monday, Wednesday, and Friday, for instance, you can work on balance and symmetry on Tuesday, do 30 minutes of stretching on Thursday, and perform a few stamina-enhancing exercises on Saturday. Change is always a good thing, and change is the basis behind the *Cross-Training* method. (See *The Skipping Trot*, p. 94.)

3. *Interval Training*. If your goal is to increase your stamina and lose a few pounds as well, then *Interval Training* is for you. This effective method alternates long periods of low-intensity exercise to ensure that you'll burn plenty of fat and calories, with short bursts of high intensity torture (we might as well call it what it really is), to ensure that your stamina will improve. One of the best things about *Interval Training* is the ease with which you can modify the exercises' challenges, something that can help you avoid boredom and prevent your muscles from adapting to the continual stress of an unchanging exercise. To modify an exercise, simply change the duration, intensity, or frequency of the high- and/or low-intensity phases. For instance, imagine a 7 minute exercise that starts with 3 minutes of low intensity, followed by 1 minute of high intensity, and then ends with another 3 minutes of low intensity. This can be easily modified to 2 minutes of *very* low intensity, followed by one minute of *very* high intensity, followed by 3 minutes of low intensity, and then finally a 1-minute, high-intensity sprint to finish. Regardless of the exercise intensity, duration, or frequency, your entire *interval* session should last at least 20 minutes. (See *The Bicycle Two-Point*, p. 94.)

Weird but true

Did you know that the term "cross-training" was originally used to describe a very unusual physical phenomenon? It referred to the fact that even if you only train your right arm or leg, your left arm or leg will also get stronger—perhaps not as strong, but stronger just the same. Connecting nerve pathways that run between your left and right limbs are responsible for this condition. Today, this phenomenon is called "collateral training," and it is often used in physical therapy situations where patients need to improve their overall strength while wearing a cast on one limb.

4. *Rider Recreation Activities*. Participating in recreational activities that have the same basic "demands" of horseback riding can be an effective and enjoyable way of improving your stamina and overall riding performance. They're also a great way to stay in riding shape when the weather makes it impossible for you to ride. There is no limit to the number or kinds of activities you can participate in, and it can be as simple as a bike ride in the park, or as complicated as a Tai Chi lesson. The best ones are *bilateral*—those that encourage both sides of the body to work equally and independently of one another. While *unilateral* activities (predominately

using one side of the body), such as tennis and racquetball, are an excellent way to stay in shape, they make one side of your body stronger, stiffer, and more coordinated than the other. So, I recommend that for every unilateral activity you do, you perform at least two bilateral activities. (See *Whoa Bo, p. 96.*)

Rider recreation activities

Below are several *rider recreation activities* that can help you *Ride Right*. Each one is matched with the riding characteristic it helps to improve.

Cross-Country Skiing	Symmetry
Cycling	Balance
Swimming	Breathing
Yoga	Body Awareness
Pilates	Coordination
Rollerblading or Skating	Rhythm
Skipping Rope	Pace Control
Dance Lessons	Grace and Suppleness
Martial Arts or Tai Chi	Reflexes
Western Line Dancing	Moving in Sequences
Gymnastics	Mental focus

Try to do an activity from each category in the next 12 months.

5. *Long Slow Distance (LSD). Long, slow-duration* and *low-intensity* riding or exercising increases your body's oxygen-delivery system and helps you maintain a healthy body by expending plenty of calories. Your body is receiving plenty of oxygen, which means that you can continue to exercise for a long time. Forty minutes of *continuous* exercise is usually the *minimum* recommended, and an 80 minute riding session made up of 20 minutes each of grooming (138 calories), walking (44 calories), trotting (118 calories), and cantering (148 calories) will burn almost 450 calories. This is about the same as playing an hour of tennis, one hour of jogging, or an hour and a half of casual cycling. (See *The Trail Ride*, p. 98.)

Frequency, Duration, and Intensity

If you've visited a gym recently, you might have overheard someone saying something like, "For the third time this week, I ran on the treadmill at level 6 for 30 minutes." Also, the last time you visited your barn, you might have overheard a rider saying, "My instructor made me sit the trot for 10 minutes without stopping, 3 times this week." While these people may not seem to have much in common, what they are saying is actually quite similar. They both referred to the *frequency* (3 times this week), *duration* (30 minutes for the runner and 10 minutes for the rider), and *intensity* (level 6 for the runner and no stirrups for the rider), of their chosen athletic event. Whenever an athlete refers to these three important things, he's referring to *stamina.*

Frequency

Frequency refers to *how often* you perform an athletic activity. While even a single, unmounted stamina session a week (in addition to your normal riding program) will help improve your stamina, you should try to schedule at least two of these sessions. In the initial stages, one to 3 weekly sessions will do the trick, but once your body's accustomed to the stress of the exercise, you can keep it challenged by

Life just isn't fair!

Humans get all the credit, but horses are jocks too! Just look at these numbers:

Calories used per hour

Activity	Horse	Rider
Walk	2,000	132
Trot	6,000	354
Canter	11,000	444

increasing the frequency to 4, or even 5 times a week. Don't forget that your body needs a rest periodically, so give it at least 2 days off each week to recover and recuperate.

Duration

Duration refers to the *length of time* you dedicate to your riding or unmounted exercise sessions and can vary greatly depending upon your goal. For instance, if you hope to improve your riding by losing a few pounds, you should exercise at a *low* intensity for at least 40 minutes without stopping. The same holds true if you're training for long-duration riding sports such as competitive trail riding, endurance, and cross-country jumping. If your riding sport requires the frequent, short bursts of intense energy like you need in team penning, cutting, and barrel racing, you should exercise at a *higher* intensity for about 20 minutes without stopping. The reason that the *exercise duration* varies is because there are two different kinds of stamina: *aerobic* and *anaerobic*.

The word *aerobic* has become one of the most commonly used terms in exercise today. While most people believe aerobic simply refers to a type of exercise class, its true definition is "in the presence of oxygen." If you want to lose weight, this definition is good to remember, because your body burns fat most efficiently in the presence of oxygen—when your lungs are able to provide your muscles

with plenty of fuel. This is why you should exercise at a low intensity for as long as 40, or even 60 minutes without stopping.

If the word *aerobic* is defined as the "in presence of oxygen," you've probably already guessed that *anaerobic* means "in the absence of oxygen." Unmounted *anaerobic* exercise

You do the math

Riding is an athletic event. You can burn up to 450 calories in 1 hour. Compare that to the other common activities. (This chart represents the approximate *number of calories* used in *1 hour* by a 30-year-old female, 5 feet 8 inches tall, 140 pounds.)

	Calories used per hour
Sleeping	60
Sitting	90
Driving a car	130
Golf (riding in cart)	220
Walking	240
Horseback riding (light)	250
Golf (carrying clubs)	290
Cycling (light)	380
Swimming (light)	380
Tennis (easy)	445
Jogging	445
Shoveling	450
Jumping rope (moderate)	650
Cycling (vigorous)	650
Jumping rope (fast)	750

For more information, and to chart your own calories according to height and weight, see caloriesperhour.com.

Exercise as if you're catching a cold

When you first notice you are coming down with a cold, you feel a few *localized* symptoms like a scratchy throat and a runny nose. Before long, however, your joints and bones begin to ache, your lungs become tight, and your head and sinuses begin to feel as if they're going to explode. When your cold has progressed this far, it's said to be *systemic,* that is, involving your entire body. Improving your mounted stamina works in much the same way. If you perform your unmounted stamina exercises once a week, you may notice a few localized improvements, but exercise two or more times a week and you'll be rewarded with many systemic benefits that spread throughout your entire body.

When you climb Mount Everest, you find it relatively easy to breathe at the base of the mountain, but as you get closer to the summit, it becomes increasingly difficult. This happens because the higher you climb this mountain, the more *anaerobic* (less oxygen-laden) the atmosphere becomes. In fact, after a certain altitude, you need to wear an oxygen mask to replace the air you left in the *aerobic* atmosphere below.

helps improve your stamina by increasing your muscles' ability to resist *lactic acid* buildup and the fatigue that always accompanies it. Since your body is working at a high intensity, your lungs are not able to deliver as much oxygen as your muscles need. As a result, you are not able to exercise (at this intensity) for much longer than 20 minutes. In time, however, your muscular and cardiovascular systems will adjust to the stress of the *oxygen debt* and you'll be able to exercise for a longer period of time before "feeling the burn." Once this happens, give yourself a pat on the back, because you've just improved your mounted stamina.

Intensity

Intensity refers to the *pace at which you perform* your riding or unmounted exercises. As I mentioned earlier, the *lower* the intensity the greater the chance of weight loss, and the *higher* the intensity the greater the gain in stamina. In order for you to receive maximum benefit from your stamina sessions, you need to elevate your heart rate into a range that's both safe and effective for your age and level of fitness. This healthy exercise range is called your *Training Heart Rate Zone (THRZ)*. You calculate your THRZ by subtracting your age from 220 to find your *maximum heart* rate, then multiplying this number by 65 and 85 percent. These two numbers will give you the upper and lower ranges of your THRZ. Every time you perform your stamina exercises, keep

your heart rate in this *safe zone*. Unless you are an elite athlete, you should never let your heart rate exceed your *maximum heart rate*.

To ensure that your heart rate remains in your *safe zone*, you need to monitor your pulse while exercising. If it's too slow, increase the exercise intensity, and if it's too fast, decrease it. To monitor your pulse, simply turn one hand over so that its palm is facing up and place the tips of the middle and index fingers from your other hand lightly in the groove that is just above where the base of your thumb connects to your wrist. You should now be able to feel your pulse. Count how many times you feel your pulse in 15 seconds, and multiply the number by 4 to get your 1-minute heart rate.

How Fit Are You?

One benchmark of overall health and fitness is your *resting heart rate*. The lower your heart rate—known also as pulse rate—the more efficient your heart is at pumping oxygenated blood throughout your body. Always record your *resting heart rate* for one full minute immediately after waking in the morning because it will increase as soon as you move around. In fact, everything—eating, walking, and even yawning—will elevate your pulse. Once you've recorded it, compare it to the benchmarks in the Sidebar, p. 89. Don't be sur-

Every time you exercise aerobically, your body uses about 70 percent fat and 30 percent blood sugar as its fuel. As long as you continue to provide your muscles with plenty of oxygen, this regular fuel mixture doesn't change much. If you deprive your muscles of oxygen however, this fuel mixture gets reversed. The problem with this new "high-octane" fuel is that it costs your body so much that you won't be able to afford enough of it to last for more than a few minutes.

prised if it starts to decrease over time as your participation in your stamina program increases. It is an indication that your heart is getting more fit, able to pump more blood with each contraction, and no longer needs to beat as often to supply your hardworking muscles with the fuel they need. This is very good news, especially when you consider that your heart will beat about 35 million times this year!

Another benchmark of overall fitness is *blood pressure*. Taking your blood pressure, a common procedure, measures the amount of pressure your blood exerts on the walls of your blood vessels and is made up of two important numbers. The upper, or first number, called the *systolic*, indicates the amount of pressure your blood exerts on your vessel walls as it's pumped away from your heart, and the bottom number, called the *diastolic*, indicates the amount of pressure your blood exerts on your vessel walls as it returns to your heart. A blood pressure reading of 120 over 80 is considered normal, while a reading exceeding 140 over 90 is considered high and suggests a need for exercise or diet modification, or perhaps blood pressure-lowering medication. The diameter of your blood vessels can shrink due to plaque deposits sticking to the inside of your blood vessels. Since your body's demand for oxygenated blood doesn't decrease, your heart is forced to pump the same amount of blood through stiffer and smaller passageways. As a result, your heart has to work harder, and the pressure on your vessel walls increases. This problem is especially critical when the blood vessels involved are the *coronary arteries*—the ones supplying oxygen to your body's most important muscle, your heart.

It is best to have a doctor measure your blood pressure, but there are personal machines on the market that can help you do it yourself on a regular basis. These gadgets, which usually measure your blood pressure at your wrist or upper arm, can be found in most shops that specialize in fitness, or regular drug stores. While they may be simple to use, their results are usually less reliable than the blood-pressure cuff your doctor uses.

Test Your Stamina with the Three-Minute Step Test

The *Three-Minute Step Test* was designed by the YMCA to measure how well your body responds to the stress of exercise and how quickly it recovers. If you're an endurance rider and think this sounds familiar, you're not mistaken. This human test is very similar to the one used to diagnose the level of fitness and exhaustion of horses participating in official endurance rides. During these events, this test, called the *cardiac recovery index*, uses a pre- and post-trot heart rate to give riders, their crew, and the vets an indication of whether or not a

STAMINA

horse is fit to carry on. Unlike this horse test, all you need to do is step up-and-down from a 12 inch high step for 3 minutes using a metronome set at 96 beats per minute to gauge your timing and rhythm—24 complete stepping cycles of up, up, down, down, each minute (figs. 9.1 A–E). Immediately after completing the *Three-Minute Step Test*, sit down and count your pulse for one full minute. Once you have your *post-exercise heart rate*, compare it to the chart below.

Sweat

Sweating is your body's way of regulating its internal temperature. It's your "built-in cold shower" when exercise heats up your hard-working body. Without the ability to sweat, your internal temperature could continue to climb to a potentially fatal high level. Sweat dissipates, which means it carries heat away from your body and its core. That is why wearing rubber suits to lose weight is such a dangerous practice. The suit encourages your body to sweat (causing you to lose weight in the form of water that you'll simply gain back the next time you drink), but the rubber holds in the heat and doesn't allow it to dissipate.

When you sweat, your skin turns a pinkish color as your blood rushes to the surface of your skin to dissipate the heat. As long as you drink plenty of fluids such as water or fruit

Post-exercise heart rate

Men	18 to 25	26 to 35	36 to 45	45 to 55	56 to 65
Excellent	<79	<81	<83	<87	<88
Good	79–89	81–89	83–96	87–97	88–98
Above average	90–99	90–99	97–103	98–105	99–106
Average	100–105	100–107	104–112	106–116	107–112
Below average	106–116	108–117	113–119	117–122	113–120
Poor	117–128	118–128	120–130	123–132	121–129
Very poor	>128	>128	>130	>132	>129
Women	**18 to 25**	**26 to 35**	**36 to 45**	**45 to 55**	**56 to 65**
Excellent	<85	<88	<90	<94	<95
Good	85–98	88–99	90–102	94–104	95–104
Above average	99–108	100–111	103–110	105–115	105–112
Average	109–117	112–119	111–118	116–120	113–118
Below average	118–126	120–126	119–128	121–126	119–128
Poor	127–140	127–138	129–140	127–135	129–139
Very poor	>140	>138	>140	>135	>139

9.1 A–E The Three-Minute Step Test

Resting heart-rate benchmarks

Below 60 is excellent
61 to 69 is good
70 to 74 is average
75 to 84 is below average
Above 84 is poor

Stephanie is performing one complete cycle of this test in these photos.

juice and let the heat escape while exercising, you'll never have to worry about your internal cold shower running dry.

Never wait for your thirst to remind you to drink because thirst is your body's way of telling you that it's already dehydrated. In fact, it's possible to lose up to 2 quarts of fluids before your thirst even kicks in. By this time, your built-in cold shower will be dangerously low on water. Not only should you be concerned about fluid loss, you should also be

thinking about the many important minerals and electrolytes your body loses through the sweating process. Since these substances, such as potassium, sodium, and calcium, are essential to the proper functioning of your body, you must replenish them along with your fluids. One good way to do this is by drinking a post-activity beverage made up of 3 parts water, 1 part orange juice, and a teaspoon of honey. You can even mix in one-half of a banana or other fruit, or purchase a prepared "sports" drink that restores your electrolyte balance. If you feel disorientated, achy, or overly lethargic when exercising or riding, chances are you're already dehydrated and your electrolyte stores are diminished. Drink plenty of fluids for a full 2 days, as this is the amount of time your body will need to fully recover.

Five Rider-Specific Stamina Exercises

Following are 5 stamina exercises to help you receive the variety of different benefits that *Circuit Training, Cross-Training, Interval Training, Rider Recreation Activities,* and *Long Slow Distance* can provide. Like all rider-specific exercises, I've designed them to imitate and exaggerate the challenges of riding while targeting your riding muscles. They also help improve your symmetry, balance, and body awareness.

EXERCISE ONE

The Balance Ball—Circuit Training

The Balance Ball is more than just a single exercise, it's a series of 5 circuit-training steps that improve the stamina of your hips, thighs, stomach, and back muscles. All you need to complete this "circuit" is about 20 minutes and a large inflatable gym ball (see *Resources,* p. 168).

Step One: Lying on your back, lift your feet so that your Achilles tendons are placed together on top of the ball. With your knees slightly bent, elbows off the floor, heels down, and hands in front of your body as if holding a pair of reins, lift your hips in an upward motion as far as you can. When you can't lift them any higher, halt for 1 second, and then lower them halfway back to the ground (figs. 9.2 A–C). Halt again for 1 second, and then lift them back up as high as you can.

When performed correctly, this exercise will mimic the motion of the posting trot. If one side of your body (especially a hip) is stronger or stiffer, the ball will likely roll toward that side whenever you post upward. You can periodically test the symmetry of your hips by lowering them toward the ground until your buttocks lightly contact it. Halt in this position and feel if one side has touched the ground before the other. If so, repeat this test often while performing the normal posting-trot motion mentioned above.

You'll find that this exercise becomes a great deal easier once you've taught your hips to move in a symmetrical manner. This portion of *The Balance Ball* can help develop and maintain a good posting-trot motion because it makes you aware of your body's tendency to post forward and to one side due to an asymmetry in your hips. Not only does it improve stamina, it also tests your symmetry and suppleness. Perform the "posting trot" in this manner for 60 seconds, and then take a 15 second rest.

Step Two: Without changing your position or the position of the ball, elevate your hips to the uppermost position, and hold them there statically to start the second portion of your circuit. Pause for a few seconds to regain your balance while keeping your head on the floor, and then slowly bend your knees so that the ball rolls toward your buttocks. Keep your heels down and your knees wide open as you move them slowly toward your chest. Once you can no longer roll the ball any further (you'll notice that your heels are now pressing into the ball), pause for 1 second and then slowly extend your knees—imagine pushing your feet into your stirrups during this movement—thus returning the ball to its original starting position. Don't lower your hips at any time; they stay raised in the upper position for the duration of this exercise (figs. 9.3 A–C). Repeat this in-and-out motion for 60 seconds and then take a 15 second rest.

Step Three: During your 15 second rest, reposition the ball so that it's between your ankles. Your knees should open and bend at about 90 degrees, and your hands should be clasped behind your head. Without pulling on your head or straining your neck, slowly lift your feet and shoulders off the ground until your knees and elbows almost touch each other. Pause in this *static* position for 1 second, and then lower your feet and shoulders until they're both about an inch off the ground (figs. 9.4 A–C). Pause again, for 1 second, and then bring them back up again. If performed correctly, you should feel your stomach, back, and inner thigh muscles starting to get tired. Repeat this sit-up motion for 60 seconds and then take a 15 second rest.

Step Four: Without changing the position of the ball as it is in *Step Three*, repeat the exercise from *Step One* exactly as described previously. Since the ball is now between your ankles and calves, you'll find the exercise more physically demanding but a little easier to balance (figs. 9.5 A–C). If the exercise is performed correctly, you once again mimic the motion of the posting trot, only this time you really feel your inner thigh muscles working hard. This is one of the best and easiest, no-need-to-go-to-the-gym exercises for improving the stamina of these muscles. Repeat this posting-trot motion for 60 seconds and then take a 15 second rest.

Step Five: During your 15 second rest, reposition the ball so that it's placed under-

9.2 A–C The Balance Ball—Step One

One complete cycle of this exercise.

neath your knees. Bend your knees at about 90 degrees, and clasp your hands behind your head. With your knees spread wide and heels down, repeat *Step Three* exactly as outlined earlier. The only difference is when you lift

9.3 A–C The Balance Ball—Step Two

A complete cycle.

9.4 A–C The Balance Ball—Step Three

Note that this exercise ends with your feet and shoulders slightly off the ground.

9.5 A–C The Balance Ball—Step Four

Here, Stephanie is repeating the Step One exercise, though this time with the ball between her legs. Her position could be improved by holding the ball at its widest point as she demonstrates in 9.4 A to C.

9.6 A–C The Balance Ball—Step Five

One complete cycle.

your feet and shoulders off the ground, you also lift the ball by squeezing tightly with your hamstrings (figs. 9.6 A–C). If you find that you cannot grip onto the ball with the back of your legs, change your ball for a smaller one. Repeat this sit-up motion for 60 seconds, and then take a 15 second rest. It's now time to start the entire circuit over again.

Each complete circuit of these 5 steps should take about 6 minutes. While 1 complete circuit may be sufficient for the first 2 weeks, try to eventually complete 3 entire circuits (without stopping) as your stamina improves.

EXERCISE TWO
The Skipping Trot—Cross-Training
The Skipping Trot is a great example of how a non-riding activity can improve your mounted performance, mimic the motion of horse and rider, and help you avoid boredom while exercising. Skipping is one of the best stamina-building exercises because it enhances your rhythm, balance, breathing, body awareness, symmetry, and mental focus. While other aerobic activities—jogging, for example—help develop your stamina, they do very little to improve other areas a rider needs to work on. If you haven't touched a skipping rope since school days, I suggest you relearn the basics before attempting this special *skip to the trot*.

Step One: With your eyes focused forward, skip normally, but instead of keeping your hips still, push them forward and backward in time with your footfalls. The opening and closing of your hips should cause your body to imitate the exact motion of the posting trot. Keep your knees bent at all times, with your kneecaps facing forward and downward, just as you do when riding (figs. 9.7 A–D).

Step Two: While *skipping to the trot*, breathe and "post" rhythmically, maintain a pace similar to that of your horse's stride, keep your eyes up, hips relaxed, and absorb the shock with your calves.

Step Three: If one side of your body is stronger or stiffer, or if you tend to "ride" too far forward or backward, you'll likely travel slowly to one side, or forward or backward. Solve this problem by drawing a square on the ground and skip within its borders. If you constantly drift in one direction, your body is slightly unbalanced or asymmetrical because a perfectly balanced and symmetrical body will stay in the center of the square. This makes this exercise a good test for symmetry, balance, and body awareness. Continue this skipping motion for 2 minutes without stopping.

Step Four: Rest for a minute, then *skip to the trot* on your *right* leg for 45 seconds. Rest for 30 seconds, and then *skip to the trot* on your *left* leg for 45 seconds. If you can skip more easily on one leg than the other, it may indicate a muscular or coordination imbalance between your right and left side. Continue to *skip the trot* 3 times a week, and you'll solve this asymmetrical problem in no time.

EXERCISE THREE
The Bicycle Two-Point—Interval Training
Bike riding is a great, unmounted exercise because it improves your stamina and balance

A few points about the two-point

The *two-point position* is a riding stance you assume when approaching a jump, riding over uncertain ground such as a rocky creek, riding in a controlled gallop across a field, or when you want to give your horse a break by taking your weight off his back. A jockey's riding position is an example of this, albeit somewhat exaggerated. To place your body in the two-point position, sit in a normal position on your horse, and then, shift your hips backward and slightly upward toward the cantle of your saddle. If done correctly, your upper body will assume a slight inclination forward, your buttocks will rise very slightly, and the majority of your weight will transfer into your inner thighs and heels. You're now ready for whatever your horse has to throw at you.

9.7 A–D
The Skipping Trot

Exaggerate your skipping position as I am doing in these photos in order to imitate the exact motion of the posting trot.

while encouraging you to use the left and right side of your body independently. One way to make biking (road or stationary) a rider-specific, *interval-training* exercise is to periodically change your position from your normal bike-riding position to one that mimics the *two-point position*. Add in a few intervals of varying pedaling intensity, and you have a perfect *interval-training program* (figs. 9.8 A & B).

Step One: Warm up your body by riding your bike in the customary, full-seat fashion for a few minutes. Once you feel ready to try the *two-point position*, find a stretch of road that is free of obstacles, flat, and relatively straight. Assume the two-point position by flattening your lower back, opening your shoulders, shifting your hips backward, bending your elbows, and placing your weight into your heels. You'll know when you have the correct amount of weight in your heels when they, and not your seat bones, support your weight. You should now have a slight space between your buttocks and the bicycle seat. Your hands should softly hold the handlebars in a supple manner and no longer support your body weight. Your shoulders are open and still, and your knees remain bent at all times. Straightening them will cause your hips to shift left and right, a movement that'll ulti-

9.8 A & B The Bicycle Two-Point Exercise

In photo A, I am riding in the regular position, and in B, the two-point position. For a good interval-training workout, alternate your regular biking position with periods of riding in the two-point position (see text on p. 94).

mately cause your shoulders to dip from side-to-side. Keep your eyes focused in front of you as if looking between your horse's ears, and breathe rhythmically. You'll probably find that riding in the two-point position feels like a 6, 7, or even 8 on the "Rate-of-Perceived-Exertion (RPE) Scale." (See Sidebar, p. 97). Ride in this position for one minute. This is your first interval of high intensity.

Step Two: Return to the normal bike-riding position for 2 minutes. This is your first rest interval. Catch your breath during this time while asking yourself questions like, "Am I placing more weight on one seat bone?" and "Does one hip feel stiffer, is one leg stronger, or is one calf more supple?" You can also use this rest interval to imitate the motion of turning your horse by turning your bike, looking in the direction you are heading toward, opening your inside shoulder slightly, and keeping your hips focused forward. If done correctly, this rest interval should only feel like an RPE of 3, 4, or 5.

Step Three: From this point on, get creative with your intervals of high and low intensity. For instance, your next high intensity interval

can consist of pedaling quickly and riding in the *two-point* position for 2 minutes (approximate RPE of 7), followed by a 3 minute rest period of riding in a normal biking position while pedaling slowly (approximate RPE of 3). To keep things interesting, you may want to make your next high intensity interval a little less strenuous by riding in the *two-point* but pedaling a little more slowly, or more so by riding in the two-point and pedaling a little faster. The same principle applies to your intervals of low intensity rest. Just alter the speed of your pedaling while riding in your normal biking position to change the intensity of these rest intervals. As you become fatigued, you may find that you need to lower the intensity or lessen the frequency of your high intensity intervals, and increase the duration and/or frequency of your low intensity rest periods. Remember that a good interval-training session will be performed in such a way that you can continue for at least 20 minutes without stopping and be varied enough to keep you interested and energetic.

EXERCISE FOUR
Whoa Bo—Rider-Recreation Activities

Kickboxing and Tae Bo have become two of the hottest and most popular exercise trends around. They are fast-paced, fun, and great ways to get into shape. I've developed a kickboxing program for riders that can help improve your balance, symmetry, breathing, body awareness, and stamina. I call this *rider recreation activity, Whoa Bo,* and all you need to enjoy it is a partner and a fun attitude.

Step One: Stand in your *normal riding position.* Your partner should be standing in the same basic position, facing you from about 2 feet away. The only difference between you and your partner is that your hands are in a rein-holding position, while hers are spread open with her palms facing you (fig. 9.9 A).

Step Two: Keeping your eyes focused forward on your partner's chest (imagine looking between your horse's ears), lightly punch her open left hand with your right hand. Now punch her open right hand with your left hand (figs. 9.9 B & C). Repeat this "straightforward" punching action 50 times, increasing the force of each punch as you go. Your weight must remain in your heels, and your elbows should remain close to your sides at all times.

Step Three: Once you've completed this short warm-up, assume the starting position again, and this time punch left, right, left, right, only. After the last punch, assume a *two-point position* by bending your knees, shifting your hips back, lowering your body, and shifting your hands forward (fig. 9.9 D). While doing this, your partner should swing her right hand in a light, sweeping motion through the place where your head was. If your head's still there, it means you didn't lower your center of gravity and you'll get a well-deserved gentle smack in the side of your head! (You might want to ask your partner to be nice for the first few attempts. After all, her turn is next.)

Step Four: Immediately after your partner finishes her swing, return to your *normal riding position* and punch left, right, left, right again. Continue to do this punch, *two-point*, punch, *normal-riding-position* motion for 3 minutes before changing roles.

Step Five: Once you have the hang of the "straightforward punch" and two-point, repeat *Steps Three* and *Four* exactly as above, only this time "turn a corner" by punching your partner's right hand with your right hand. As you do this, open your left shoulder slightly and imagine that you're asking your horse for

Rate-of-perceived-exertion (RPE) scale

The easiest way to gauge intensity levels of your intervals is to use the *Rate of Perceived Exertion (RPE)*. Using the RPE, you rate the intensity of an interval on a scale from 1 to 10. A 1 might be equivalent to reading this book in a big comfy chair, and a 10, like sprinting the last mile of a marathon.

Riding-intensity scale

Activity	Intensity Level
Sitting in the saddle at a halt or walk.	1
Turning your horse in 10 meter circles at the walk.	2
A gentle posting trot on a comfortable horse.	3
Cantering an easy-to-control horse.	4
A posting trot on a bouncy horse.	5
Cantering a somewhat-difficult-to-control horse.	6
Jumping multiple jumps in a row without resting.	7
Barrel racing at full speed.	8
Playing a fast chukka of polo.	9
Galloping the last mile of a 100 mile endurance race.	10

Using this scale, levels 6 and below indicate *aerobic* exercise, and levels 7 and above indicate *anaerobic* exercise.

a turn to the left. Punch your partner's left hand with your left hand while slightly opening your right shoulder and imagining you're asking your horse to turn right. Regardless of which hand is punching, your hips should face forward, and your weight should be equally distributed in both heels (figs. 9.9 E & F).

Step Six: This exercise can be made even more challenging by jumping forward after each two-point position. In this case, the cadence is left, right, left, right, two-point, jump, left, right, left, right, two-point, jump, and so on. When doing this exercise, always remember to keep your weight in your heels, open your knees, keep your hands in front of your body, and most importantly, have fun.

The Bicycle Two-Point and *Whoa Bo* are two good examples of how you can turn normal recreation activities into good, rider-specific exercises. Knowing what you know now about exercise specificity, spend a few minutes thinking about your favorite non-equestrian sport, and see if you can make it a little more

A) Starting position B and C) Forward punching D) Two-point E and F) Side-to-side punching position.

rider-specific. Changing your regular golf stance or reception position in volleyball to a *two-point position* are two such ways to accomplish this (fig. 9.10). If you think hard enough and keep an open mind, you'll surely find many ways to change your favorite pastime into good training tools for your riding.

EXERCISE FIVE
The Trail Ride—Long Slow Distance

For the last unmounted stamina exercise, *The Trail Ride*, you're going to use the *Stable*

Board again. Because it exaggerates the symmetry and balance challenges of a normal exercise, it certainly has a place in your stamina program. All you need for this exercise, in addition to your board, are about 20 minutes and a great imagination.

Start by standing on your *Stable Board* in your *normal riding position* and imagine that you're taking a long trail ride through the forest or along the beach. Whatever you envision yourself doing on your ride should be imitated on your board. Start by warming up your

9.10 Rider Recreation Activities

As you've seen, cycling and Whoa Bo are regular sporting activities that can be well adapted to help your riding. Golf is another candidate, as my two-point position demonstrates in this photo.

imaginary horse at a walk for 5 minutes, walking as you did in the *Riding Lesson* (see p. 53, and remember the *agitator-arm* motion of your hips). Imagine turning your horse to the left and right as he makes his way down the twisty trail. After 5 minutes, do a transition to the "posting" or "sitting trot," and continue for another 5 minutes. Periodically, pretend that you're jumping your horse over stumps or fallen trees. Do this by jumping up and down on the board as you did in *The Jumping Test* (see p. 56). All this "trotting" is bound to make you a little tired, so rest for 2 minutes by riding in your *two-point position*. This tends to be the easiest position on the board because your center of gravity is lower than it is at the walk, trot, or canter. Once rested, do a transition to the "canter" (changing leads periodically, as you should do while trail riding) and "canter" for 5 minutes, once again jumping over any imaginary obstacles that come your way. Finish this exercise by "cooling your horse down" by walking him for the final 3 minutes.

❈

CHAPTER TEN

FLEXIBILITY

At one time or another you've probably ridden a horse that felt a little stiff or crooked, even after you'd taken the time to warm him up properly. While you might have assumed that he was just naturally inflexible, there's a possibility that something else was causing this. That "something else" could have been your own stiff or crooked body! So, before you ride, your body must be properly prepared for the work to come. You know the importance of this when it comes to your horse. After all, you don't jump on and take off at a full gallop without first warming him up. Learn to treat your body with the same respect. When you do, there's a good

hibited way, and perhaps the greatest benefit, enables you to move in a supple manner. The reason that this is so important is because a lack of suppleness in one body part always interferes with suppleness in other body parts.

Test this out by clenching your hands into the tightest fists possible. (Clenching is usually caused by poor suppleness.) As you squeeze harder and harder, you'll feel muscular tension crawl up into your forearms, elbows, biceps, shoulders, and neck. You might even clench your teeth together, tighten your facial muscles, or hold your breath. Do the same thing with your toes. As you clench them together, you'll notice that the stiffness runs up into your calves, thighs, inner thighs, and hips. Relax your toes, and then clench them again, only this time, pay close attention to your knees. Chances are the stiffness created in your hips and inner thighs

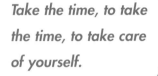

Take the time, to take the time, to take care of yourself.

Monkey see — monkey do!

Your horse often develops the same imperfections as you. For instance, if poor neck suppleness causes you to jut your chin forward while riding, he'll likely jut his chin too. To prove this to yourself, stand in a relaxed position, place one hand on the muscles of your lower back, and briskly jut your chin and shoulders forward. As you do, you'll feel your lower back, buttock, and hamstring muscles tighten and your hips tilt forward and lock. When your lower body is stiff and your hips are locked, you won't be able to follow the rhythmic motion of your horse, and your horse will react by hollowing his back and lifting his head and neck, thus causing his chin to stick out. A simple lack of suppleness in your neck area is enough to affect the suppleness of your entire body and cause your horse to mirror your imperfection.

chance that much of your horse's stiffness or crookedness will magically disappear.

Rider flexibility refers to the range of motion, as well as the elasticity of your tendons, ligaments, and muscles. Good flexibility protects your body against injury, allows your muscles to work in proper coordination, permits your joints to move in a free and unin-

will actually cause them to pinch together. This test does a good job of showing how something as innocent as clenching your toes can have a very negative effect on your entire riding performance.

Another unusual way to show the relationship between stiff hips and pinching knees is to imagine the stance you take when you have to wait to urinate (back rounded and knees and inner thighs squeezing together hard). The muscular tension created in your hips makes it very hard for you to maintain supple knees and inner thighs. If you've ever ridden while needing to urinate, you've felt the impossibility of riding in a supple and relaxed manner in such a situation.

Benefits of Warming Up and Stretching

Warming up and *stretching* are two activities that should go hand-in-hand when preparing your body for the physical stress of riding. Warming up increases the heat and consequent suppleness of your muscles, and stretching increases muscle and joint flexibility by gently extending them. When used together, these important and non-time-consuming techniques help you to achieve the same results you strive for when warming up and stretching your horse. The following is a list of the many benefits a pre-ride warm-up and stretching program can have on your riding performance.

Posture
Asking your horse to round his back by contracting his abdominal muscles and stretching his back during his warm-up and stretch period is a good way of developing good equine posture. As a rider, you can also attain good upper body posture by warming up and stretching your own chest muscles. Once these muscles become supple and flexible, they'll let your shoulders open and your back flatten naturally. One of the easiest ways to warm up your chest muscles is to simply hold your arms parallel to the ground and rotate them—in one direction and then the other—in circles of varying sizes (see p. 117).

Suppleness
Asking your horse to soften his neck and accept the bit during his warm-up and stretch period is a good way of ensuring balance, suppleness, and communication. You can accomplish the same thing by heating and softening your own muscles through increased blood flow. *The Ball Lift* warm-up (see p. 105) is a great example of the kind of movement that can help you accomplish this.

Left and Right Balance
Turning your horse left and right during his warm-up, or asking him to stretch to the left and right—with the aid of an apple or other treat—before mounting, is a good way of improving his symmetry. You can also improve your symmetry by performing similar stretches on both sides prior to riding (see p. 110).

Range of Motion
Asking your horse to lengthen his stride (by bringing his hindquarters well underneath his body) during his warm-up is a good way to improve his range of motion. Do the same thing by moving your joints in large supple movements prior to riding. (See *The Inner Thigh Stretch*, p. 115).

Rider Performance
As mentioned earlier, a good warm-up and stretching program helps you eliminate the first 10 minutes or so of any riding session. You'll then be able to *Ride Right* for the full lesson without having to wonder why your joints are so creaky. One great warm-up to help loosen your joints is called *The Ball Twist* (see p. 105).

Horse Performance

When you improve your flexibility, you improve the suppleness of your horse, as well. For instance, if you have stiff hips, your horse may develop stiff hips because each time he tries to lengthen his stride by bringing his hindquarters under his body, his hips will hit a wall created by your unyielding hips. If this continues to happen, he'll likely learn to shorten his stride, an action that'll decrease his hips' range of motion and flexibility—the last thing you want. But when you *improve* your hips' suppleness, he'll increase his stride, and in doing so, his own suppleness. (See *The Hip Stretch* on p. 111.)

Injury Prevention

Cold muscles, tendons, and ligaments, are more injury-prone because they don't absorb shock as well as warm ones. When your muscles are warmed-up prior to riding, they become elastic and pliable. For instance, stretching your calf muscles will help your body absorb shock that would otherwise be transferred up your spine. (See *The Calf Stretch*, p. 115, using the mounting block. It is a great way to increase the elasticity of your lower legs.)

Resistance to Fatigue

Cold muscles don't accept oxygen well and are, therefore, more prone to the burning pain of *lactic acid* buildup. Warm muscles accept oxygen easily and can delay the onset of this painful condition. As a result, a good warm-up program can actually help you ride for a longer time without feeling the burn. (See *The Ball Pass* warm-up on p. 106.)

Weight Control

Believe it or not, warming up can even help your body burn fat. Each time you start exercising, fat is released into your bloodstream. If your muscles are warm, they can use this fat as fuel, but if they're cold, the "door" to your muscles remains closed, and the fat is forced elsewhere—like inside your arteries or thighs. All 5 of the stamina-enhancing exercises (p. 90), and all 5 of the *Equi-Librium* exercises (p. 53) are great choices to help you achieve this.

Warming Up

If the term "warm-up" leads you to believe that you need only jump into a Jacuzzi or sauna for a few minutes before riding, you'd better prepare yourself for a disappointment. While these modalities certainly heat the surface of your body, they do very little for the deep core temperature of your muscles, tendons, and ligaments. This is where the *neural*

Which comes first... the warm-up or the stretch?

Take a piece of red licorice. This licorice is very elastic and pliable when warm, but after putting it in the freezer for a few hours, it is cold and brittle. Instead of being supple and pliable, it breaks before it bends or stretches. Your muscles and ligaments work in very much the same way. When they're warm, they're flexible, supple, and stretchable, but when they're cold, they're stiff, fragile, and resist all efforts to change shape. Just like the cold licorice that breaks into many pieces, your cold muscles, tendons, and ligaments will *strain* or *sprain* if you try to bend them. A *strain* is the overstretching or bending of a cold muscle or tendon, and a *sprain* is the overstretching or bending of a cold ligament.

You can avoid these painful problems by always warming muscles up before stretching. Since even something as simple as sitting in your car while driving to the barn can cause your muscles and ligaments to become cold, it's important to remember this simple rule. The good news is that once your muscles are heated up, they'll remain warm for the duration of your ride so you can stretch them after the warm-up, during the ride, and even afterward.

Talk without stuttering

Your reins connect your hands to your horse's mouth, and through these reins, you transmit your thoughts, commands, and desires. If your hands, wrists, arms, elbows, and shoulders are stiff, your reins are not able to follow your horse's mouth in a supple manner (causing the reins to go slack, tight, slack, and so on) and the communication traveling down them becomes interrupted and choppy (A and B). When you talk to your horse in this way, he may understand the general idea of what you're trying to convey, but the choppy manner in which you're speaking (much like stuttering when you talk) may cause him to become frustrated and unsure of your intentions. You can ensure that your thoughts, commands, and desires are clearly understood by making sure that your hands, wrists, arms, elbows, and shoulders are supple (C and D). *The Ball Twist* and *The Ball Pass* warm-up exercises on p. 105, and the *mental image for supple arms* on p. 161, can help you achieve this.

10.1 A–D "Talking" without Stuttering—Rein Communication

In A and B, Erin is demonstrating rein tension alternating from tight to slack. When this happens, communication fails, and the horse has a difficult time understanding the rider's aids. In C, Stephanie has very good contact and a nice hand and rein position. See the straight line joining her elbow and hand with her horse's mouth. In D, Erin's hand position is too low and "tucked into her pocket," thus limiting its usefulness.

and *chemical* changes take place to supple your muscles, tendons, and ligaments, and where your muscle fibers must slide past one another. To accomplish deep muscle heating, you can choose from three different warm-up techniques, *sport-specific*, *general*, or *combined*.

Warm-Up Techniques
Sport-Specific
This warm-up technique prepares your body for the stresses of riding by having you perform a slowed-down version of the actual activity. A polo player, for instance, can spend 4 or 5 minutes preparing for a chukka by slowly swinging his arms and twisting his torso in the same manner he use during the game. Likewise, a dressage rider or jumper can prepare for her sport by trotting and cantering on the *Stable Board* for a few minutes before riding. You can think of this warm-up as a gentle dress rehearsal of what's about to come. *Sport-specific* warm-ups are very effective at preparing your mind and body for the demands of riding because they ensure your riding muscles are ready to work while putting you in a riding state of mind.

General
This kind of warm-up doesn't take into consideration the exercise specificity, it simply sets out to prepare your body by moving as many of your muscles as possible. A brisk walk or brief jog before riding is a good example. Add 5 or 10 minutes of grooming, and you'll have effectively warmed up all your muscles and raised your heart rate, something that'll help your lungs provide your muscles with the oxygen they'll need.

Combined
Before riding, why not take the time to complete both a short *general* and *sport-specific* warm-up. Wake your muscles up, for example, by taking a brisk walk around the barn, followed by a few minutes of "trotting" and "cantering" on the *Stable Board*.

Regardless of which technique you choose, the more intensely you plan to ride, the longer your warm-up will need to be. If you only plan to go for a short hack, 5 minutes should do the trick. Increase this by a few extra minutes if you intend to ride longer.

Rider-Specific, Warm-up Exercises
Every exercise in this book can be used as a *sport-specific* warm-up. Simply slow them down a little so that you're performing them at intensities lower than the level for strength or stamina benefits. A 3 or 4 on the *Rate of Perceived Exertion* (*RPE*) scale (p. 197), or a heart rate between 50 and 60 percent of your maximum heart rate (p. 86) is the recommended level for warming up. When you warm up at this intensity, your breathing should be a little more rapid than normal, but not as fast as during the actual exercise.

The Ball Lift
To prepare your *lower body*, stand in your *normal riding position* and place a small ball between your calves, just above your ankle-bones (see *Resources*, p. 168). Shift your weight onto your left leg, put your right heel down, and slowly roll the ball up and down your left leg by lifting your right knee and flexing your right hip (figs. 10.4 A–D). Repeat this "lifting leg-aid motion" 20 times without losing your balance or letting your right foot touch the ground, and then change legs and do it on the right leg.

The Ball Twist
To warm up the *upper-body*, stand back-to-back with a partner, facing forward in a *normal riding position*. Without shifting your hips to the side, open your left shoulder and pass a ball to your partner's right hand. Once she has the ball, rotate your upper bodies so

Are you a rusty hinge?

When a joint is stiff, it acts like a rusty hinge and causes other parts of your body to move inadvertently. A common riding problem is when your hip joint is stiff and your lower legs move every time your upper body moves. When your upper body falls forward, your unchanged hip angle causes your legs to move backward, and when you lean back, your legs move forward. Stiff hips cause most leg-positioning problems.

To see what this feels like and how it can affect your riding position, stand on your left leg, and lean as far forward as possible. As you lean, your right leg will automatically swing backward. Lean as far backward as possible. Your right leg will swing forward. This is exactly what happens to your legs if you ride with rusty hips.

10.3 A & B Stiff Hips

Stephanie demonstrates the need for a proper warm-up. These leg positions can happen when your stiff hip joints cause your legs to move inadvertently—not what you want when riding.

that she can pass the ball back to you on your right side. Continue to pass the ball back and forth in this manner for one minute, and then change directions (figs. 10.5 A–E). Always remember to breathe rhythmically, keep your knees bent, and hips facing forward. You know you're doing this warm-up correctly when your stomach, back, thigh, and shoulder muscles all begin to heat up.

The Ball Pass
If you want to warm up your *upper* and *lower*

body at the same time, stand 6 feet away from your partner in your *normal riding position* and pass a ball back and forth (a 6 pound medicine ball works well) by extending your hands forward as if releasing your horse's head (see *Resources,* p. 168). Lower your body into a *two-point position* as you throw the ball, and wait in this position until it's thrown back to you. As you receive the ball, return to your normal riding position for 1 second, and then repeat the throw in the same position as before. When you catch the ball, don't look at it, but keep your eyes focused forward as if looking between your horse's ears, and use your body awareness to "sense" where it is (figs. 10.6 A–D).

Take the time to look at the many different exercises in the *balance*, *symmetry*, *strength*, and *stamina* sections of this book. Pick one exercise from each section, as well as one of the three exercises above, and make a point of trying them prior to your next riding lesson. From time-to-time, go back to these sections, and choose four new exercises. By doing this, you'll not only continue to challenge your body, you'll also avoid getting bored with the same old warm-up exercise.

Stretching

Unlike warm-up exercises that are *dynamic* in nature, stretching is almost always *static*. You can improve your performance and prevent injury by stretching your muscles after you've taken the time to warm them up. If you don't have the time to complete a full warm-up in addition to your stretches, you should use whatever time you have to do a good warm-up. Once you've started to ride, you can

10.4 A–D The Ball Lift

This exercise prepares your lower body for riding. Photo A shows the starting position, B to D show Erin rolling the ball up and down her left leg by lifting her right knee and flexing her right hip. Repeat 20 times, then change legs.

This exercise prepares your upper body. Passing the ball as shown will "heat up" your stomach, back, thigh, and shoulder muscles.

Test your suppleness with the "skin jiggle" test

If you're like most people, feeling whatever extra skin you have jiggling around may not sound very tempting, but try this test anyway because it's a great way to tell what suppleness feels like. While riding, relax your muscles until you can feel your skin start to jiggle. Initially, you may only feel a slight skin jiggle on the back of your arms or chest, but as your body awareness becomes more acute and your muscles become more supple, you should be able to feel your lower back, buttocks, and thighs begin to jiggle as well. This is what suppleness feels like!

10.6 A–D The Ball Pass

To warm up your upper and lower body at the same time, pass the ball back and forth as shown. Note you alternate between the normal riding position and the two-point position.

Make the time

You know that warming up before riding is a good idea, so find the time to do it. There are 1,440 minutes in every day, so 5 minutes isn't such a big deal.

stretch during your lesson, as well as afterward. If you have a little extra time, but not enough for a full warm-up and stretching session, do a brief, general warm-up (1 minute of jumping jacks, for instance) and then complete all your stretches. Your muscles should only be stretched after they've had the chance to warm up a little. There are several other guidelines you should follow when stretching.

The stiff, supple, stiff rule

Not only is overall suppleness important, the left and right sides of your body must be equally flexible and supple. If one side of your body—or one limb—is stiffer, give it a little more attention by stretching it first for 15 seconds, and then stretch your supple side. Repeat the stretch once again on your stiff side only. In this way, your stiff side receives twice as much attention as your supple side, which will eventually help bring both sides into symmetrical suppleness.

Stretching Guidelines

No bouncing. Always hold your body in a relaxed, static position because bouncing tight muscles causes injury. These innocent little movements cause a *rebound reflex*, which can lead to microscopic tearing of your muscle fibers. Avoid this by slowly stretching until you feel a slight ache, called your *end range*.

Hold each stretch for at least 15 seconds. As soon as you start a stretch, your muscles become convinced you're trying to tear them off the bone. As a result, they'll actually contract slightly to protect themselves. After a few seconds, however, they respond and begin to relax. If you hold each stretch for less than 15 seconds, your muscles may only contract and not reach the relaxation stage, which is the phase that supples them. By holding each stretch for more than 15 seconds, you can ensure that they relax, lengthen, and become more flexible.

Find the good ache. A lot of people think that stretching needs to be painful. Nothing could be further from the truth. Always stop deepening the stretch once you feel a light sort of general ache. It's not necessary to continue any further than this *end range*, or what I like to call the *good ache*. If during your 15 second hold, the good ache starts to dissipate, gently deepen the stretch. Once you've recaptured the original good ache, relax, and hold the new deeper stretch for the remainder of the time.

Breathe rhythmically. Gently exhale each time you *deepen* your stretch, and when you've reached a *good ache* remind yourself to breathe rhythmically. Holding your breath will increase the muscular tension in your body, the exact opposite effect of what you're trying to achieve.

Make it convenient. Even though all riders know the benefit of a pre-ride stretch, most still don't do it. Improve your chances of making stretching a part of your riding program by making it as convenient as possible. You can do this by performing only standing and sitting stretches. Horse barns often aren't the cleanest places on earth, so having to stretch while lying on the ground is probably not going to encourage you.

No snap, crackle and pop. If during a stretch, you feel or hear any of these sounds, or if you feel a sharp, deep pain, stop the stretch immediately—it's not for you. If you feel an intense burning sensation, you've likely just stretched too far. This is called your *stretch threshold* and you should lessen the stretch until the pain disappears. You can never stretch too little, but you can certainly stretch too far.

Monitor your progress. Measuring your stretching performance is a good way to tell if your flexibility is improving. For instance, if you can touch your toes this week and the ground next week, you know that your hamstring stretches are paying off.

Eight Rider-Specific Stretches
Before riding, you should stretch the muscles in your hips, lower back, shoulders, inner thighs, calves, hamstrings, quadriceps, and chest because these are the body areas that are most active, and each muscle group should

receive equal attention because stiffness in one usually causes stiffness in others (see fig. 8.1). In the following text, you'll find one stretch for each of these important groups, as well as a simple test you can use to determine each muscle's flexibility. While most of the stretches can be done just prior to mounting, there are a few flexibility tests that require you to lie on the ground and should probably be done in the comfort of your own home. Don't forget to warm up first.

Hip Stretch and Flexibility Test

Good hip flexibility allows you to achieve a deep, supple seat, tilt your pelvis forward during motions such as one you use to do a half-halt, follow the rhythmic motion of your horse's body, and permit your legs and upper body to work independently of one another.

Stretch your hips. I suggest two different hip stretches. One stretches the front of the hips, and the second stretches the sides. To begin, stand in a lunge position, and gently stretch your back leg's hip forward (figs. 10.7 A & B). You should feel a good stretch in the front part of your hips. Hold this stretch for 15 or more seconds, and then change legs. Stretch the sides of your hips by standing in an upright position and shifting your hips to one side with that arm over your head, until you feel a nice stretch in the side of that hip (the so-called "love handle" area). Hold for 15 or more seconds, and change sides (figs. 10.8 A & B).

Test hip flexibility. In a sitting position (a

10.7 A & B Front Hip Stretches

10.8 A & B Side Hip Stretches

10.9 A–D
Test Hip Flexibility

In photos A and B, Stephanie is demonstrating a supple right hip. She presses gently down on her knee to give it a little extra stretch. C and D show that her left hip is not so supple—this leg is not parallel to the ground. However, from this position, she can carefully give it a stretch to increase its flexibility.

mounting block works well for this), cross your right leg so that its foot is sitting comfortably on your left knee. The soft space below your right anklebone should be resting in the soft space just above your left kneecap. You have *good* flexibility if your upper leg is parallel to the ground, *average* flexibility if it's slightly elevated, and *poor* flexibility if the leg is very elevated (figs. 10.9 A–D). Test both sides to check whether or not your hips are symmetrically supple. If they are not, stretch them using the *Stiff, Supple, Stiff Rule* (see Sidebar, p. 110).

Lower Back Stretch and Flexibility Test
Good lower back flexibility allows your torso to remain erect and supple and your body and legs to work independently of one another while following the rhythmic motion of your horse. It also plays a major role in creating the *pelvic tilt*, a movement that makes such riding skills as the half-halt and deep-seated canter possible.

Stretch your lower back. Standing in a relaxed manner, slowly bend your knees and collapse your body until your back is rounded, your knees slightly bent, and your chin tucked into your chest (fig. 10.10) Hold this position for 15 or more seconds, and then slowly return to a starting position. While doing so, imagine that you have heavy weights in each hand, keep your chin tucked into your chest, and uncurl your back, one vertebra at a time. When done correctly, you'll feel your lower back stretch in both the curled and uncurled positions.

Test lower back flexibility. Lie on the ground beside a mirror that extends to the floor. While watching yourself, slowly bend one knee, and bring it as close to your chest as possible. Without the assistance of your arms, make note of how closely you can bring your knee to your chest before your other knee leaves the floor. Your goal is to be able to close the angle between your back and thigh to at least 60 degrees. If you cannot, your back is too stiff. Take this test on both sides to see if it's symmetrically supple. If it's not, stretch it using the *Stiff, Supple, Stiff Rule* until it becomes so.

10.10 Lower Back Stretch

Shoulder Stretch and Flexibility Test

Flexibility of the shoulder girdle promotes good riding posture and balance. Supple shoulders that open without muscular tension also make it possible for you to deliver smooth, effective, and coordinated rein aids.

Stretch your shoulders. Standing in your *normal riding position*, grasp your right elbow with your left hand, and gently pull your right arm across the front of your chest. Stop pulling once you feel a *good ache* in the back or side of your right shoulder (figs. 10.11 A & B). Hold this position for 15 or more seconds, and then change arms. Be careful not to overstretch your shoulders as this

can cause pain. You should only feel a good ache in the muscle and not a sharp point pain.

Test shoulder flexibility. Stand in your normal riding position, place your right hand behind your lower back and reach upward, and place your left hand behind your neck and reach downward. You have good right shoulder flexibility if you can grasp your hands together, average flexibility if you can touch fingertips, and poor flexibility if you can't touch at all. Take this test on both sides to see if your shoulders are symmetrically supple (figs. 10.12 A–D). If they're not, stretch them using the *Stiff, Supple, Stiff Rule* until they become so.

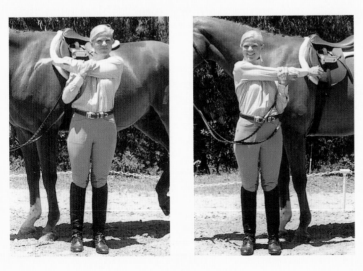

10.11 A & B
Shoulder Stretch

Grasp an elbow with the other hand, and gently pull your arm across the front of your chest.

10.12 A–D
Test Shoulder Flexibility

In this exercise, you are testing the shoulder flexibility of the "underneath" or lower arm as seen from the back. In A and B, Stephanie is showing the suppleness in her left shoulder because she is able to grasp her hands behind her back. C and D show her inability to touch one hand to another, demonstrating that her right shoulder is very tight.

10.13 A–C Inner Thigh Stretch

10.14 A–C Calf Stretch

Inner Thigh Stretch and Test

Inner thigh or *adductor* flexibility allows you to wrap your legs around the barrel-shaped body of your horse, protect your inner thighs against muscle strains, maintain a deep seat in the saddle, and deliver coordinated and independent leg aids.

Stretch your inner thigh muscles. Stand in a relaxed manner with your legs spread wide apart and your toes facing straight forward. Rotate your torso so that you're facing your right foot and try to touch both of your middle fingers to your right toe without bending your knees. Stop once you feel a *good ache* in your inner thigh, and hold the stretch for 15 or more seconds. Slowly return to a starting position, and repeat the stretch for your left leg. Before returning to a full standing position, bend straight forward and touch the ground midway between your legs (figs. 10.13 A–C). Do you feel more of a stretch in one leg? Hold this stretch for 15 or more seconds, and then slowly return to a standing position.

Test your inner thigh muscles. Perform the inner thigh stretch again, only this time, make note of how far you can stretch before reaching the *good ache.* You have *good* adductor flexibility if you can touch the palms of your hands to the ground, *average* adductor flexi-

bility if you can touch both middle fingers to your toes, and *poor adductor* flexibility if you can only touch your middle fingers to your shins. Take this test on both sides to see if your *adductors* are symmetrically supple. If they're not, stretch them using the *Stiff, Supple, Stiff Rule.*

Calf Stretch and Flexibility Test

Calf flexibility helps you lower your body weight into your heels and absorb shock. When you can, you're able to attain a longer leg, make more competent leg aids, improve your balance, develop a deeper seat, and prevent injury.

Stretch your calves. Find a raised surface such as the first step of a mounting block, and place the balls of your feet on it. The rest of your feet, including your heels, should be hanging in midair. With the help of gravity, lower your body weight into your right heel until you feel a good ache. Relax, and hold this position for 15 or more seconds, then repeat the stretch with your left heel. Is one calf more flexible than the other? Then, stretch both calves at once (figs. 10.14 A–C).

Test your calves. Stand in front of a mirror that extends to the floor, lift one foot off the ground, and flex it so that it's in a heels-down

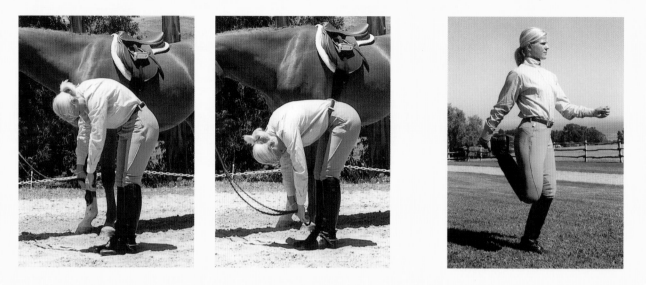

position. When you can flex it no more, make note of the angle between your foot and your shin. You have good calf suppleness if this angle is less than 70 degrees; average calf flexibility if the angle is less than 80 degrees; and poor flexibility if the angle is more than 80 degrees. You may want to ask a friend to help measure this angle with a protractor. Take this test on both sides to see if your calves are symmetrically supple. If they're not, stretch them using the *Stiff, Supple, Stiff Rule*.

Hamstrings Stretch and Flexibility Test
Flexible hamstrings make it possible for you to apply leg aids, mold your legs around the barrel-shaped body of your horse, change the position of your legs, soften your lower back, and protect your lower torso and legs against injury.

Stretch your hamstrings. If you can remember your junior high school gym class, you can probably remember doing the well-known stretch called *touching your toes*. You bend at the waist, and try to touch your toes without bending your knees. Stop reaching as soon as you feel a *good ache* (even if you haven't reached your toes yet), and hold the stretch for 15 or more seconds (figs. 10.15 A & B).

Test your hamstrings. Perform the hamstring stretch as above, only this time, cross your right leg in front of your left. Bend at your waist, and try to touch your feet. You have good left hamstring flexibility if you can touch your palms to the ground; average left hamstring flexibility if you can touch your toes; and poor left hamstring flexibility if you can't touch your toes. Slowly return to a standing position, and repeat the test with your left foot crossed over in front of your right. Take this test on both sides to see if your hamstrings are symmetrically supple. If they're not, stretch them using the *Stiff, Supple, Stiff Rule*.

Quadriceps Stretch and Flexibility Test
Flexible thighs are important because they increase the range of motion and suppleness of your hips and lower legs. When the quadriceps muscles are stiff, you lock your hips, pinch with your knees, and lift your heels. Suppleness of these muscles is, therefore, important for many movements in riding, such as the posting trot, canter, two-point position, and jumping.

Stretch your quadriceps. I call this stretch *The Flamingo* because you must stand on one foot to perform it. Stand on your left leg, bend your right

10.17 A & B
Chest Stretch

In photo A, Stephanie stretches her right chest and in B, she stretches her left side.

knee, and gently pull on your right foot with your right hand until it touches your buttocks. Stop briefly to regain your balance, and then gently pull your right leg backward until you feel a *good ache* in the front of your right thigh. Keep your knees close together, and don't lean forward. Remain in this position for 15 or more seconds, and then repeat the stretch for your left leg. You can hold onto your stirrup leather or saddle flap, or place your free hand in front of your body as if bridging your reins (fig. 10.16).

Test your quadriceps. Repeat *The Flamingo*, only this time make note of how far you can pull your leg behind your back before you feel the *good ache*. In order for the test to be accurate, you must keep your knees close together and not lean forward. You have *good* quadriceps flexibility if you can pull your leg back 4 inches behind your other leg, *average* quadriceps flexibility if you can pull your leg back 2 inches, and *poor* quadriceps flexibility if you can pull your leg back less than 2 inches. Take this test on both sides to see if your thighs are symmetrically supple. If they're not, stretch them using the *Stiff, Supple, Stiff Rule*.

Chest Stretch and Flexibility Test
Flexible chest muscles allow your shoulders to open naturally and without tension. When they're tense, they have a tendency to pull and round your shoulders forward. For this reason, they play an important role in posture and balance.

Stretch your chest. Stand on the left side of your horse. To stretch your right side, start facing forward, and with your right hand holding the back of the flap or cantle of your saddle, rotate your body so your hips, shoulders, and feet are pointing directly away from the horse. You should now feel a *good ache* in the armpit, elbow, forearm, and even palm of your right arm. Hold this position for 15 or more seconds. To stretch the left side of your chest, start by holding the pommel or front flap of your saddle with your left arm while facing the back of your horse, and rotate your body in a similar fashion (figs. 10.17 A & B).

Test your chest. Repeat the chest stretch, only this time, take note of how far your body rotates before you feel the *good ache*. You have good chest flexibility if your body and feet rotate more than 90 degrees; average chest flexibility if your body and feet rotate 90 degrees; and poor chest flexibility if your body and feet rotate less than 90 degrees. Take this test on both sides to see if your chest is symmetrically supple. If it's not, stretch it using the *Stiff, Supple, Stiff Rule*.

The Ultimate Hip Suppleness Exercise

This exercise teaches you to eliminate hip tension by relaxing the muscles that control urination and defecation. The rationale behind it is that the small ring of muscles that stops urine flow controls all the muscular tension in the front of your hips. (If you've had a baby, you've used these muscles to perform Kegel exercises, and if you haven't, these are the muscles you tighten very quickly when someone unexpectedly walks into the bathroom.) Another small ring of muscles that makes up your anal sphincter controls all the muscular tension in the back of your hips. As unusual as it may sound, you can virtually eliminate all hip stiffness by simply relaxing these two small rings of muscles while riding. This is true for both women and men.

In addition to the suppling effect, this exercise can also improve your sense of balance by lowering your center of gravity and widening your base of support. If you want to feel how these two rings of muscles can release hip tension and improve your balance, try this simple exercise. Stand in your *normal riding position*, contract both rings of muscles as hard as you can, and move your hips forward and backward as if imitating the motion of the canter. As you do this, you'll find that your hips are completely locked, and your midsection is as stiff as a board. You are also probably holding your breath and feeling a great deal of tension throughout your entire body.

Once you've felt this uncomfortable feeling, close your eyes, and completely relax your pelvic and anal sphincter muscles. Like a person who has lost her sight, your other senses will be heightened when your eyes are closed, and you'll feel incredible suppleness in your hips. Once again, imitate the motion of the canter, only this time "force" these two small rings of muscles to remain relaxed. I use the oxymoron "forced relaxation" because unlike most relaxation, you can actually achieve a deeper level of release and suppleness by feeling as if you're forcing yourself to urinate and defecate. With your eyes still closed, and feeling the deep hip relaxation, perform four separate releases of your anal sphincter muscles.

If done correctly, each release should make your body feel as if it's getting lower and lower (lowering your center of gravity), and wider and wider (giving you a wider base of support). Your buttocks and inner thighs will now feel as if they could gently fill every nook and cranny on your saddle. Imitate the motion of the canter one final time, and feel how easy it is to perform this motion when your hips are free of tension. Try "cantering" on both leads by advancing your right and left pants' pockets toward a wall while keeping your weight in your heels. Regardless of the motion you attempt, you'll find it's always easier and more efficient when you take the time to relax and unhinge your rusty hips.

The next time you ride, relax the two rings of muscles while your horse walks. Feel your hips move gently in motion with his body. Then, tighten these muscles and notice how your body becomes as stiff as a board. In the beginning, this technique may be difficult to perform at any gait other than the walk, but keep trying and soon you'll be able to ride with perfectly supple hips at the walk, trot, and canter.

PART FOUR

FRAME AND YOUR FUTURE

ENSURE THAT YOU ENJOY THE CHALLENGES AND REWARDS of riding for many years to come by regularly exercising, resting, eating well (and by "well," I mean in a healthful way), and warming up and stretching before riding. These habits will keep your body fit, and will go a long way to keeping you free from injury.

Why are rider-specific exercises important?

Grade the following items of concern in the order of importance. Retake the test every few months to see if your reasons for exercising change.

Body weight	_____
Balance	_____
Symmetry	_____
Body awareness	_____
Flexibility	_____
Reflexes	_____
Injury prevention	_____
Posture	_____
To treat your horse better	_____
To ride longer without fatigue	_____

CHAPTER ELEVEN

WHAT TO EXPECT

You didn't learn to ride overnight, and you probably won't become strong, fit, flexible or perfectly balanced and symmetrical overnight, either. However, if you practice the exercises in this book, maintain a positive attitude, and warm up and stretch before you ride, you can improve your frame in a very short time. Since this will have a big impact on your horse's performance and happiness, it will be well worth the time and effort. So, just how long should it take? The following schedule of progress will give you a better idea of what to expect.

After One Week

When exercising, you should expect to feel a bit of localized muscle soreness, but not pain. You should simply feel a slight ache in your muscles indicating that you've been challenging your body to improve itself. Anytime you feel a sharp or shooting pain, stop immediately, and rest the affected body part. If you take the time to warm up and stretch before, during, and after each exercise, you'll likely never experience this kind of discomfort. During the first week, you might also feel a little frustration when trying to perform the exercises perfectly. The exercises, like riding, are not simple, but don't worry because this frustration is normal and should only motivate you to try harder in the future. Regardless of muscle soreness or frustration, you'll almost surely leave each exercise session feeling more refreshed, fit, supple, balanced, and symmetrical.

After One Month

Your dedication and patience is paying off because the exercises are getting easier, and your riding is getting better. You're still not perfect, but you know you're closer to perfection than before, and your horse is definitely noticing the difference in your riding. You see a little more muscle definition and feel less fatigue. These positive changes have inspired you to continue working on your own body as a way of improving the body of your horse.

After Three Months

Your unmounted exercises and pre-ride stretches have now become a way of life. You no longer need to force yourself to do them because your improved fitness and happier horse are more than enough to motivate you. The exercises and stretches now hold a very important place in your overall riding program. You finish each session feeling more fit, energetic, and positive than the last. Your improved strength, stamina, and suppleness, as well as your enhanced symmetry, balance, and body awareness, are all having a very positive effect on your riding.

After Six Months

You're now an exercise and stretching "junkie." Your new and improved body and riding skills have changed the way that you look at your horse and riding life in general. You take greater pride in yourself and contribute much of your horse's improvement to your new and improved frame. Missing an exercise session is something to be avoided. You leave each session feeling great about yourself and your progress. Your body is now more fit, toned, and supple than ever and is still improving. Your horse loves you for making the effort and probably wishes that you had done it earlier.

Ten Tricks for Staying on Track

Regardless of whether your goals are based on symmetry, balance, body awareness, breathing, strength, stamina, or flexibility, you can ensure you'll reach them with these ten simple tricks.

1. Think "gradual." Trying to fix all of your imperfections quickly will only lead to disappointment. In fact, it's likely that an overzealous attitude will convince you that self-improvement is too hard, and you will give up. So, set a few reasonable goals, and start out slowly by working on your rider biomechanics first. Once you feel comfortable with these exercises, then challenge yourself with the conditioning ones.

2. Expect to feel your imperfections. Following your first day of unmounted exercises, you may ride much "worse" than before! While this may be unexpected (after all, you'd like to think that all your hard work makes you feel better in the saddle), it's actually very normal. The reason you might feel uncomfortable is because you are riding with an incredibly heightened sense of body awareness. While just yesterday you were riding in ignorant bliss, completely unaware of your mounted imperfections, today you are feeling each and every one of them. This is an incredibly positive step because you can correct what you can feel.

3. Set many short-term goals. Setting several easy-to-attain goals is a great motivator. Monitor your progress by recording a few goals in a journal, and take pride in yourself when you accomplish one by whipping out a big red marker and crossing it off the list. You can even reward yourself (and your horse) with a gift such as a new halter or a bag of horse cookies.

4. Develop a good schedule. Jot down your exercise and stretching sessions in a date book or calendar, and stick to them like any other important appointment. If a chosen time turns out to be inconvenient, change it so that it better meets your needs. The best time for the *biomechanical* and *flexibility* exercises is just before riding; your body will still be feeling the heightened sense of awareness and suppleness when you mount. *Strength* and *stamina-enhancing* exercises can rob your body of much needed energy so you might want to consider scheduling them on a day when you don't ride. Regardless of the exercises, always try to schedule them for the same time each day. They stand a much better chance of becoming a regular part of your daily routine.

5. Change your exercises regularly. We all crave change. If you repeat the same program day in and day out, you'll soon get bored and lose interest. In addition, when your muscles become accustomed to the stress of unvarying exercise, they adapt and stop improving. Avoid this by mixing stamina-enhancing days with balance-enhancing days, hard days with easy days, and even unmounted days with mounted ones. When it comes to self-improvement, variety will help you stay motivated and on track.

6. Exercise with a riding friend. Just knowing that you have an exercise appointment with a riding peer is often enough to get you over the "I'm-not-in-the-mood" bridge. Make one of you the "horse" and the other the "rider." When working on the *Stable Board*, the rider will be the one "trotting" or "cantering," and the horse will be the person who is holding the rider's hands and telling her that she's looking down, pinching with her knees, or holding her breath.

7. Do the 5 minute compromise. Try this trick on days when you feel as if you've been run over by your horse and can't bear the thought of exercise. Tell yourself that you'll exercise for 5 minutes only, and if after that time you're still not in the mood, you'll "pack your bags" and leave. I call this a "trick," because in most cases, these 5 minutes will boost your energy so much you have no problem finishing the entire session.

8. Prepare to succeed. If you've had difficulty achieving your self-improvement goals, tell yourself that this time you're going to succeed. If you think you're going to fail, you won't work as hard because you already have a built-in excuse. Visualize yourself, not only as a rider, but as an athlete, and remind yourself how much it means to your horse that you're learning to *Ride Right*.

9. Think of your horse. Even if your exercises

or stretches only take a few minutes, spend this time thinking about your horse: what you learned at your most recent lesson, what you hope to accomplish today, and how you intend to do it. Asking yourself these important questions while preparing yourself physically will ensure that you're prepared mentally as well.

10. Have fun!

⁕

CHAPTER TWELVE

INJURY PREVENTION

While *exercise-related injuries* can be caused by exercising or riding too vigorously, they can also be caused by poor posture, neglecting to warm up or stretch, and not allowing your body to rest and recover between sessions. If you try too hard, and convince yourself that more is better, you risk suffering an injury that'll interfere with your riding enjoyment and performance. Allowing yourself to be fueled by the fear that you're not attaining your goals fast enough can also have the same disappointing result.

With riding accidents, the only solution is prevention. Horses are large, cumbersome animals, and it's unreasonable to believe that you can completely avoid riding-related injuries by simply never falling off or getting stepped on again. The only way you can really prepare and protect your body is to be strong, supple, and fit. When your body is in peak physical condition, it can better resist and recover from injuries. The following *Exercise-Safety Rules* will help you achieve this.

Exercise-Safety Rules

1. Vary your exercises. If you perform the same exercises day after day, your muscles, bones, and joints will break down from the constant and unchanging physical stress. Avoid this by alternating *biomechanical* and *conditioning* sessions. You can even vary your *conditioning* exercises by alternating between *circuit, interval, long slow distance,* and *cross-training* in your *stamina* sessions.

2. Give your muscles time to recuperate. The best thing you can do for your hard-working muscles, bones, and joints is to let them recover from the stress you're putting them through. In fact, you should take your recuperation periods just as seriously as your

> ## You can never predict, only prepare!
> Horses are unpredictable animals, so riding accidents and injuries will always be a part of our great sport. You don't know when, or even if they'll happen, but if they do, you can recover quickly by keeping your body fit and healthy.

exercise and riding periods. When you're *strength training,* always give your muscles at least 48 hours of rest before working them again, and never exercise the same muscle group two days in a row. Your muscles don't care that "bikini season" is only a few weeks away, they only care that they have enough time to take care of themselves!

3. Rest actively. You can rest your muscles *actively* with a relaxing walk or a brisk grooming session, or *passively* by watching television. While *passive* rest is better than no rest at all, it doesn't encourage blood to flow to your recovering muscles as does *active* rest. Since blood delivers oxygen and removes waste products left behind after exercise, active rest is the best. As long as it doesn't elevate your heart rate past 50 percent of your maximum, it'll be welcome and effective relief for your recovering muscles.

4. Exercise with good form and function. When performing any exercise or stretch in this book, always do so using good posture and proper breathing. Never hold your breath, let your muscles bounce between the contraction and relaxation phase, or lift heavy weights. If you have to sacrifice good form and breathing, there's a good chance the exercise intensity is too high. Remember that cheating won't make you strong, it'll only make you sorry!

5. *Exercise with a partner.* A riding friend can help you avoid injury by reminding you to use good form, help you complete any difficult efforts (this is called *spotting* in fitness jargon), and make the exercises safe. Placing her foot against your *Stable Board* so that it can't slide while you're standing on it is a good example.

6. *Listen to your body.* If you feel what appears to be the beginning of an injury, immediately stop the exercise and reevaluate your program. You're an athlete, and your greatest asset is your body, so don't ignore what it's telling you or you might end up breaking it. Listen to it. More than likely, it's saying something like, "Hey, lay off, I'm exhausted!"

Delayed Muscle Soreness

When you subject your body to a physical activity that's very intense or unfamiliar, it's not uncommon to feel some muscle tightness or soreness the following day or days. This sensation is called *delayed muscle soreness* (DMS), because unlike lactic-acid pain, which occurs during the activity, or the immediate pain you feel after your horse stands on your foot, it actually waits a day or two to arrive. It also differs from normal pain. Instead of hurting a great deal in the beginning and decreasing as it heals, *DMS* doesn't hurt at all in the beginning, but gets worse as the muscles heal. The reason that *DMS* reacts so differently is that unlike normal pain, it's not really related to an injury at all. While it's associated with some microscopic tearing of your muscle tissue, it's actually considered more of a healing process (giving off a slight ache) than a true injury type of pain. The best thing about *DMS* is that it provides a constant physical reminder that your muscles are still in the "damage-and-repair" phase and, therefore, not ready to go back to work yet. Given enough time to rest and recuperate, the microscopic tears in your muscle fibers will heal themselves so that they're stronger than before.

Common Riding Injuries

Riding is a great way to stay in shape (as well as spend a few hours with one of the few beings in this world that doesn't talk back to you), but it can lead to *exercise-related injury*. Some of the most common riding injuries and the ways to avoid them are listed below.

1. *Hip and knee.* Most of these injuries are caused by the unnatural way that your hips, legs, and knees must position themselves to lie flat against the barrel-shaped body of your horse. The dynamic opening and closing of your hip angle, as well as the constant muscular tension in your knee area, also contribute to the problem. This discomfort is especially common in riders with pre-existing hip or knee

problems and women with loose joints and knock-knees. The good news is that a rider-specific exercise program can help solve many of these problems by strengthening and supporting the muscles, tendons, and ligaments of your knees, hips, lower back, and abdominal areas. Pain can be alleviated by combining *stretches* for the inside of your knees, buttocks, hamstrings, and front of the hips, (see *Hip Stretch*, p. 111 and *Inner Thigh Stretch*, p. 115) with *strengthening* exercises for your lower back, abdominals, and outer legs (see *Symmetry Stomach*, p. 77 and *The Ball Twist*, p. 105).

A pain in the neck

If you feel discomfort during or after exercising, take this quiz to find out if the pain you're feeling is *delayed muscle soreness (DMS)*, or something more serious.

1. When did you first notice the pain?
a) During or immediately after exercising
b) 24 to 48 hours after exercising

2. Where is the pain?
a) Near or inside a joint
b) Inside the muscle itself

3. What does the pain feel like?
a) A sharp or burning type
b) A deep, localized type of ache in the muscle

4. What happens when you do light exercise?
a) It feels the same or even worse
b) It begins to feel a little better

5. How is flexibility in the affected area?
a) A great deal more limited than before
b) About the same, or slightly less than before

If most of your answers are "b," you are likely suffering a case of *DMS*. Stop exercising until the pain disappears, but provide lots of *active rest, warm-up activities, stretching,* and *rider-recreation activities*.

If most of your answers are "a," you could be suffering from an *exercise-related injury*. Stop exercising, and contact your doctor.

2. *Lower back.* Poor posture, bad balance, and weak abdominal or back muscles cause lower back problems. The constant jarring, concussion, and micro-vibrations your body sustains while riding a 1000 pound animal (doing his best to imitate the movement of a jackhammer) also play a major role in creating discomfort. Your spine is made up of 33 separate vertebrae, each one stacked on top of another with small, fluid-filled *discs* separating them. These tiny discs protect your spine by absorbing the shock that's transmitted from your horse into your spinal column.

When you ride with poor posture, greater compression and pressure is exerted on one side of your spine, causing the fluid inside one or more of the *inter-vertebral discs* to get pushed toward the back or side. Once this happens, the affected disc will bulge out like a small balloon and put pressure on the nerves that run to and from your spine. A sharp pain radiating from your lower back through your buttocks, leg, and foot is usually the result.

You can avoid suffering this uncomfortable condition (often referred to as *sciatica* or a *herniated disc*) by increasing the strength and flexibility of your lower back, hips, hamstrings, and abdominal muscles, and improving your posture and balance. Every *Stable Board* exercise in this book helps you strengthen these muscles because standing on an unstable surface forces all of them to contract in a safe manner. This is why *balance boards* are so commonly used by physical therapists. Regardless of whether these professionals are trying to strengthen or heal a back, hip, abdominal, knee, or ankle problem, chances are they use a balance board to help you reach your goal. With the exception of *The Calf Stretch*, every stretch and warm-up exercise can help you supple these important body areas, and in doing so, help you avoid suffering from a lower back injury.

3. *Neck and upper back injuries.* Most of these injuries are due to poor posture, stiff, upper back muscles, and mental tension. Often, these conditions combine to round your shoulders and jut your chin forward. While this may not sound all that serious, it can create a domino effect, resulting in discomfort and pain throughout your entire upper torso. When you ride with rounded shoulders or a jutting chin, your head (which weighs as much as 15 pounds), protrudes further forward than normal. Once it's no longer centered over your neck, the muscles of your spine, back, and shoulders are forced to work extra hard to keep it there. This, in turn, causes your shoulders to round even more, a "frame-flaw" that eventually interferes with your balance and symmetry and causes your lower back and hip muscles to become stiff and tired. The result is usually diminished shoulder mobility, decreased suppleness (and mastery of rein aids), and stiff hips. Exercises that strengthen the muscles of your upper back, especially the ones located between your shoulder blades (*The Rein Aid*, p. 79, combined with *The Chest Stretch*, p. 117), can help you avoid or overcome this painful condition.

4. *Compression fractures, pulled muscles, strains and sprains, shoulder tendonitis, and arthritis.* The majority of these injuries are caused by poor mounted posture, constant spinal concussion, weak muscles, bad balance, and asymmetry. Injuries in this group are not usually caused by flaws in your riding but a lack of warming up and stretching, and also by riding accidents or twisting an ankle while dismounting.

Injury Treatment

It's your job to make sure an injury hinders your riding for the shortest amount of time possible. Regardless of the injury, *R.I.C.E.*

(the athletic equivalent to chicken soup or an apple a day) will help your body heal from stress and discomfort.

Rest

Allow the injured area to rest, repair, and recuperate by immobilizing it. In a serious case (a broken bone), your doctor guarantees you rest the affected body part by immobilizing it in a cast. Your veterinarian does much the same thing when she prescribes complete stall rest to a horse that has suffered an injury such as a pulled tendon. Most riding-related injuries don't need to be immobilized in a cast, but it's still a good idea to avoid using the injured area until it's fully healed. Slings and special support bandages are two common ways of achieving this.

Ice it

Apply ice to an injury using these two tricks:

1. Take a frozen bag of peas, and tap it lightly against a counter until it's no longer frozen solid. You'll now be able to wrap it around oddly shaped body parts, such as an ankle, knee, or elbow.

2. Fill ten small, paper water cups halfway with tap water, and place them in the freezer. Once frozen, remove one, and tear away the top portion of the cup so that a half-inch of ice is exposed. You can now massage the ice directly onto the injury while holding the dry portion of the paper cup.

Ice

Localized inflammation (fluid) and redness is greatly responsible for the pain you feel. The best way to decrease this swelling is to apply ice to the affected area. When the injured body part is exposed to cold, blood and other fluids are forced away from the site, thereby decreasing the inflammation. Beware of frostbite. Never let the ice stay in contact with your skin for longer than 20 minutes. Remove it for 20 minutes before applying it again. Repeat this "20-on" and "20-off" program as long as comfortably possible for the first 24 to 48 hours. Afterward, the inflammation process will have passed, and you can start applying heat to the area. This floods the area with plenty of blood so that it can carry away any remaining toxins or waste products.

Compression

The third way to reduce inflammation is to apply slight pressure, called *compression*, to the area. When applying a compression bandage to yourself (or your horse, for that matter), ensure that it is only "snug," not "tight." You should be able to slide one or two fingers between the body part and the bandage. If it's too tight, remove it and wrap it again less tightly. Keep the bandage in place until the area is healed, but be sure to remove it every few hours for at least 20 minutes to allow blood and other fluids to circulate through the area. If you're prone to repetitive injuries, or have naturally weak joints, you might want to consider purchasing an athletic support bandage— much like an equine sports-medicine boot— and keep it in place while riding or exercising.

Get red in the face!

When you're in a hot climate, your capillaries dilate, allowing your blood to come to the surface of your skin and release heat, and your skin turns pink. This is called *vasodilation*. When the weather turns cold, the capillaries seal themselves off so that your blood can stay in your body's core where it's nice and warm, and your exposed skin turns white. This is called *vasoconstriction* and is exactly what you're attempting to do when you apply ice to the site of an injury.

Elevation

You can also help reduce inflammation by *elevating* an injured body part above the height of your heart. This works best for limbs because it's often uncomfortable—if not impossible—to elevate a lower back, hip, or abdominal injury. For instance, if you sprain your ankle, apply ice and a compression bandage, then elevate and rest your foot so that it's higher than your chest. Lying on your back with your foot propped up on a pillow is one way to do this. Regardless of which part of your limb you injure, *elevation* can help drain the fluids away from it.

As seen on TV

You've probably seen a professional athlete applying an ice pack to his elbow or knee while his teammates continue to play the game. This athlete realizes he's injured and must apply *R.I.C.E.* before he can play again.

Riding-related injuries can take a considerable amount of time to heal so be patient and respect your body during the healing process. Rushing your recovery can cause you to re-injure the area, only more severely the second time around. Remember that you're an athlete just like the ones you see on TV, so when injured, respect your body by applying *R.I.C.E.*

CHAPTER THIRTEEN

HEALTHY EATING

We have been conditioned to think that there's something especially cute about a chubby little pony going around with a child on top. This cuteness disappears, however, when the pony's weight interferes with his health and performance. The same rule applies to you. You know the importance of feeding your horse a healthy diet, so learn to do the same thing for yourself. Eating a diet rich in energy-providing foods, vitamins, minerals, and electrolytes, and keeping to a good weight will ensure you'll be able to keep up with your well-nourished horse. Being overweight often causes poor flexibility, lack of stamina, incomplete leg contact, an insecure seat, and difficulty sensing the horse's movement.

You can provide your body with the energy it needs by eating a variety of foods including grains, vegetables, fruits, legumes, lean meats, eggs, and dairy products. When your diet includes a healthy balance of these foods, you are eating a *balanced diet*. Eat too many fatty foods, junk food, or refined sugars that you find in many cookies and pastries, and your balanced diet gets very quickly thrown "out of balance."

Balanced Diet

Grains

Depending on your size, *The Healthy Eating Pyramid* devised by Dr. Walter Willett and his colleagues at the Harvard School of Public Health suggests you eat a serving of whole grain foods—such as some breads, rice, pasta, and cereals—at most meals. One serving size of grain is equivalent to about 1 slice of bread, 1 ounce of ready to eat cold cereal, or ½ cup of cooked cereal, rice, or pasta. Grains, especially whole wheat, are very "rider-friendly" because they're a great source of minerals, energy-producing carbohydrates, and B-vitamins.

Vegetables

Eat fresh vegetables in abundance, such as broccoli, carrots, spinach, green beans, onions, asparagus, cauliflower, and cabbage. A single vegetable serving is equivalent to about 1 cup of raw, leafy vegetables, a

Blame technology

Four reasons for obesity

Television. Leisure activities are more sedentary since this invention. This trend continues today with more of it: satellite TV, cable, pay-per-view, videos, and DVDs.

Computer. This machine is responsible for the elimination of many jobs that involved some exercise, as well as (thanks to the Internet) providing another sedentary leisure activity.

Car. Unlike a hundred years ago when you and your horse often did the work, you no longer exercise to move from place to place.

Fast Food. "Improved" taste (in most cases caused by the addition of fats and sugars), ability to order food that's "ready in a minute" (and requires no cleanup afterward), and the convenience of the microwave all make it easier to eat more, and to eat poorly.

single medium-sized carrot, an equivalent piece of broccoli or cauliflower, ½ cup of other vegetables—cooked or chopped raw—or ¾ cup of vegetable juice. Vegetables are easily digestible, low in fat, high in fiber, and rich in vitamins, antioxidants, minerals, and water content. While eating a variety of different vegetables is recommended, always make sure to eat a few that are dark green or orange in color as studies show that these vegetables have the highest levels of nutrients and antioxidants.

Fruits

A juicy apple isn't just a snack or reward for a horse, it's also a very healthy food for you. You should eat 2 or 3 daily fruit servings. An average serving size of fruit includes a handful of grapes or berries, a medium apple, pear, kiwi, mango, nectarine, peach, banana, orange, ¾ cup of pure fruit juice, or ½ cup of chopped, cooked, or canned fruit. All fruit is low in fat and high in nutrients, vitamins, water content, fiber, electrolytes, and energy-producing carbohydrates.

Dairy

To be sure your muscles and bones remain strong and healthy, eat 1 or 2 daily servings of *low-fat*, *skim*, or *fat-free* dairy products such as yogurt, milk, cottage cheese, cream cheese, sour cream, and hard cheese. A single serving size is equivalent to 1 cup of milk, cottage cheese, or yogurt, 1 ½ ounces of hard cheese, or 2 ounces of processed cheese. Dairy products provide your body with plenty of muscle and bone-building protein and calcium. These two elements play a major role in helping your body remain strong and "injury proof," something that'll come in handy the next time your horse stands on your foot or you go "dirt-surfing."

Red Meat, Fish, Poultry, Eggs, Nuts, and Legumes

Use red meat sparingly. Eat 0 to 2 daily servings (2 or 3 ounces cooked) of skinless poultry, fish, or eggs. Eat nuts and legumes 1 to 3 times daily. One-half cup of cooked dry beans—kidney or brown beans—peas, or lentils, 1 egg, or 2 tablespoons of peanut butter each count as 1 ounce of lean meat. A diet that's rich in legumes, with some lean meat, poultry, fish, and eggs is an excellent source of protein, iron, and zinc. Meat, poultry and eggs are rich in muscle-building protein; fish is high in cholesterol-lowering, Omega-3 fatty acids; and legumes are very high in calcium and B-vitamins.

White Rice, White Bread, Potatoes, Pasta, and Sweets

Use sparingly.

Carbohydrates, Protein, and Fat

Food is made up of *carbohydrates*, *protein*, and *fat*. These substances are the building blocks that fuel your body. I'll discuss them individually.

Carbohydrates

Carbohydrates are the sugars and starches that provide your main source of energy. Unlike protein and fat, some carbohydrates pass directly from your intestines into your bloodstream. As a result, your muscles receive a short-term, yet almost immediate boost of energy. Other carbohydrates are absorbed more slowly into your bloodstream and provide your body with the long-term fuel it needs for lengthy rides. Overindulgence of carbohydrates should be avoided because they can leave you feeling bloated and fat. You can comfortably reap their energy-producing benefits by limiting them to about 55 percent of your total daily caloric allowance. There are two different kinds of carbohydrates.

Simple carbohydrates found in foods such as vegetables, fruit, and sweets (table sugar, honey, syrup, candy, sodas, chocolate) provide your body with quick boosts of energy because they're very easily absorbed into your bloodstream. With the exception of vegetables, these foods can be described as "sugary." Simple carbohydrates such as candy and chocolate (often called "empty" calories because they contain little or no nutrients, fiber, minerals, or vitamins) should make up only a *very small* portion of your daily diet.

Complex carbohydrates found in foods such as whole grain breads and cereals, pasta, potatoes, and legumes, provide your body with long-term energy because they're more slowly absorbed into your bloodstream. In order for this to happen, they must first take a "trip" to your liver to be broken down into smaller pieces called *glucose*. Once broken down, they're absorbed into your bloodstream and carried to your muscles to be used as fuel. With few exceptions, most of these foods can be described as "starchy."

Complex carbohydrates, which deliver a great deal of energy over an extended time, should make up the bulk of your daily carbohydrate consumption. If preparing for a strenuous riding event such as an endurance or competitive trail ride, or even a dressage, jumping, or three-day event, you should probably "load up" on your complex carbohydrates a day or two in advance. Once the show arrives, you'll be sure to have plenty of energy. Note that loading up on simple carbohydrates has just the opposite effect. Instead of creating a long-term boost of energy, eating a "sugary" snack will give you a very brief boost, but to no avail because it causes a dramatic drop in your blood sugar, and consequently, your energy level. This occurs because your muscles are starved of the fuel they need to continue work-

ing, and you feel as if you can no longer go on. Weakness, shaky hands, deep hunger, and sweating are some symptoms of this *carbohydrate crash*. The change in your body's insulin level is responsible for this kind of weakness.

Protein
Protein also provides energy, but is mainly responsible for helping your body build and maintain strong muscles, and healthy skin and hair. When a protein enters your body, it's broken down into many small pieces called *amino acids*, which become the building blocks of your muscles and other body tissues. In order for your body to function at its best, it must receive a total of 22 different amino acids. When you eat a balanced diet, your body can manufacture 14 of these amino

> ## The battle of the bulge
> In 1900, 15 percent of Americans were obese. Eighty years later, the figure increased to more than 25 percent. Today, obesity affects 1 in every 3 Americans over the age of 20.

acids all by itself. The remaining 8, however, must be obtained from your diet by eating foods rich in 2 different types of protein.

Complete proteins are the best of all because they naturally contain all 22 essential amino acids. Foods rich in complex proteins—all meat, egg, and dairy products—always come from animal sources.

Incomplete proteins are those that do *not* contain all 22 essential amino acids. Foods rich in incomplete proteins—bread, rice, cereals, and potatoes—usually originate from other than animal sources.

The most complete sources of protein are found in lean meats, poultry, fish, cheese, milk, and other dairy products. Eggs have the distinction of containing the highest quality protein of all. Unfortunately, while all these sources contain the most protein, they're also high in fat content. Since sources of animal fat (with the exception of fish, egg whites, and skinned, white meat poultry) are less beneficial than fat found in vegetables and grains, you should limit the amount of animal protein in your diet. So just how can you get the benefit of complete proteins without eating too much fat in protein foods? The answer to this intriguing question is something called *complementing* your proteins.

You can *complement proteins* by eating a combination of several incomplete proteins. When you blend two incomplete proteins, (rice and beans, for example), they combine to form *one single complete protein*. When eaten alone, they can't deliver all 22 essential amino acids but when eaten together, the two incomplete proteins form one complete protein. Other examples of complement proteins are wheat products plus beans; nuts plus grains; potatoes plus milk products; and even whole-wheat bread plus peanut butter.

Approximately 25 percent of your daily caloric intake should come from protein. To help calculate how many daily grams of protein your body needs, multiply your weight in pounds by 0.36. Increase this multiplier to 0.50 if you participate in a strength-training program or if you are pregnant, and to 0.75 if you're healing from a broken bone or exercising in an extremely intense manner. Don't exceed these amounts, because too much protein causes your kidneys to work overtime, which can lead to nausea, fatigue, dizziness, and dehydration. To find the protein content of a food simply look at the nutrition label on its package. If the food you're eating doesn't come with a nutrition label, you can still find its protein content by looking in a book on healthy eating that includes nutrition levels—including calories and fat.

Fat

Fat is the third kind of fuel that powers your body. Gram for gram it has more than twice the calories of carbohydrates and protein. Since fat is so high in calories, it is able to pro-

vide your body with a great deal of *stored energy*, the kind of energy your body uses after you've been riding or exercising for a long period of time. When your carbohydrate and protein "fuel tanks" run empty, your body switches over to its stored "fat tanks" so that it can continue working. Without this fuel reserve, you'd run out of gas before completing your long-duration activity. In addition to its role in energy production, fat also plays an important role in insulating your body against temperature extremes, cushioning your internal organs, storing vitamins A, D, E, and K, and keeping your skin and hair in good repair.

While *some* dietary fat is healthy, *too much* interferes with your body's ability to function well. An increased susceptibility to serious diseases, such as diabetes, cancer, and heart disease is the price you may pay for excessive fat consumption. For this reason, you should not only limit your fat intake to about 20 percent of your daily calories, but you should

How much fat is too much?

"Too much" is when a food gets more than 20 percent of its calories from fat. Read the nutrition label on its package and multiply the fat grams by 20. If the result is greater than the total number of calories, it's too "fatty."

Example

A cookie with 6 grams of fat and 100 calories is too "fatty" because:

6 grams of fat x 20 = 120 (more than the 100 calories)

also completely avoid eating the most dangerous high fat proteins. The good news is that while some fat is a risk to health, there is actually fat that is good for you. There are three categories:

Saturated fat poses a big risk to your heart and health because it is associated with elevated levels of blood cholesterol, plaque deposits on the inside of blood vessels that lead to coronary artery disease, and other serious illnesses like cancer, diabetes, and obesity. This fat is generally found in well-marbled meat, dairy products such as butter or lard, and tropical oils such as palm and coconut.

Trans and *hydrogenated fats* are two more unhealthy fats. These so-called "designer fats" are found in fat-reduced and processed foods such as margarine and low-fat snacks. While these products may seem attractive if trying to lose weight, you should make an effort to limit them in your diet by replacing them with naturally low-fat fruits and vegetables, for example. There's mounting evidence they might be even worse for your health than saturated fat.

Unsaturated fat is the "healthiest" of all fat, because it does not cause an increase in blood cholesterol levels. In fact, studies credit this kind of fat with promoting an actual decrease in cholesterol levels, which protects your body from diseases such as coronary heart disease, cancer, diabetes, and obesity. There are two different kinds of unsaturated fats, the best being *monounsaturated,* found in plant-based oils including olive and canola, and the other being *polyunsaturated,* found in vegetable-based oils such as corn, sunflower, cottonseed, and safflower.

Unsaturated fats rather than *saturated, trans,* and *hydrogenated fats* should make up the bulk of your daily fat calories—20 percent of total calories. Limit the three "bad" fats to less than 7 percent of your total daily calories so that the remaining 13 percent can come from the "good" unsaturated fats. The best way to do this is to limit the amount of fried foods, processed snacks, and marbled red meat in your diet.

Cholesterol

Cholesterol is another substance that has a negative effect on your overall health. Pure cholesterol is an odorless, white, powdery substance that you can neither taste nor see in food. While some cholesterol is important for the healthy functioning of your body, too much can cause serious problems, such as heart disease.

You're an animal product

Cholesterol is found in all animal products, including dairy, meat, poultry, and seafood. Even if you don't eat these foods, your body will still contain plenty of cholesterol because your liver produces it. After all, you're an animal product, too.

The cholesterol in your body is measured in milligrams per deciliter of blood. To find out if you're at risk from high cholesterol, ask your doctor to perform a cholesterol profile of your blood. Cholesterol readings can vary greatly from day-to-day (called *biologic variation*) because of changes in your diet, exercise, stress, and medications, so request two or three separate readings and use the average as your true reading. A reading of less than 200 mg/dl is optimum, 200 to 239 mg/dl is above average health risk, and more than 240 mg/dl is high risk.

Cholesterol and fat are similar in that neither mixes well with water. In order for these substances to be carried by your blood, they must first be wrapped in a thin layer of protein. The result of this wrapping is a waterproof substance called a *lipoprotein.* There are two kinds of lipoproteins, one beneficial, the other not.

High Density Lipoprotein (HDL) contains a great deal of protein and very little cholesterol. This "good" cholesterol can actually remove the non-beneficial lipoprotein from your blood and, therefore, prevent the plaque buildup on your blood vessels' walls. Increasing the amount of this lipoprotein is so good for your body that your risk of heart disease decreases as your *HDL* level increases.

Low Density Lipoprotein (LDL) contains a great deal of cholesterol and very little protein. This unhealthy cholesterol, which is responsible for depositing the fatty plaques on the inside of your vessel walls, is closely related to heart disease.

Behavioral and dietary modifications such as lowering your *saturated* fat intake to 7 percent of your total calories, increasing your physical activity, not smoking, and reducing your daily cholesterol intake to less than 300 mg, can help improve your cholesterol profile. Stress management techniques also help because stress is known to decrease the blood flow to your liver, the site where cholesterol is processed for removal from your body. One last trick to help rid your body of cholesterol is to increase your consumption of dietary fiber. This will ensure that cholesterol-containing substances, such as bile, can bind to the fiber and be "piggybacked" out of your body via its own cholesterol disposal system.

Metabolism

How many calories must you eat to maintain a healthy and strong body? To answer this question, you need know how many calories your body needs to simply survive. This is called your *resting metabolic rate* (*RMR*) (see Sidebar, p. 137) and refers to the number of calories your body expends on vital functions such as breathing, heat production, and the beating of your heart. Your *RMR* also takes into consideration something called *specific dynamic action* (*SDA*), or the number of calories your body expends to digest, absorb, transport, and metabolize your food. Once you've calculated your *RMR*, add to it the number of calories you expend while performing physical activities such as riding, grooming, walking, and exercising. There is a sample list of energy expenditures for these physical activities on page 185 in the *Stamina* section of this book. This new total is called your *active metabolic rate* (*AMR*) and refers to the number of calories your body will need to ingest to maintain your current weight. (See Steps One to Three in the sidebars on page 137 to calculate calories needed to maintain and lose weight.) You can make sure that you don't gain weight by doing two important things.

Remain active. Physical exercise is one of the only proven ways to increase your *RMR*. Aerobic exercises tend to be better than anaerobic, and strength training seems to be best of all. Anything that improves the quality of your muscles improves your *RMR* because it takes more calories to maintain and repair a pound of muscle than a pound of fat. As long as you continue to exercise, your body will continue to burn calories at a higher rate, 24 hours a day, 7 days a week.

Eat "healthy." Eating a balanced diet is the second way to avoid gaining weight. If you ingest *more* calories than you expend, you gain weight, and if you ingest *fewer* calories than you expend, you lose weight. Since each pound of fat contains 3,500 calories, you can lose a pound a fat by expending 3,500 calories more than you ingest. Unfortunately, every time you ingest 3,500 calories more than you expend, you'll also gain a pound of fat.

Losing Weight

Your safe *weight loss goal* will not be lower than your *RMR*. You might also have noticed that active individuals get to eat more than inactive individuals. Obviously, this is because they need the added calories so they can continue to exercise or ride at their current level of intensity. When trying to lose weight, avoid doing so in an extreme way because you likely won't reach your goal any faster. There are several reasons for this.

1. If you severely limit your daily caloric intake, you become weak and no longer have the energy to exercise. As a result, you decrease the number of calories your body expends, and your "starving" yourself will be for naught.

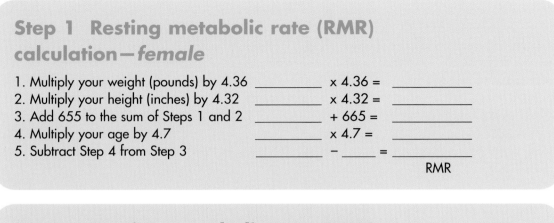

Step 1   Resting metabolic rate (RMR) calculation—*female*

1. Multiply your weight (pounds) by 4.36 _____ x 4.36 = _____
2. Multiply your height (inches) by 4.32 _____ x 4.32 = _____
3. Add 655 to the sum of Steps 1 and 2 _____ + 665 = _____
4. Multiply your age by 4.7 _____ x 4.7 = _____
5. Subtract Step 4 from Step 3 _____ − _____ = _____

RMR

Step 1   Resting metabolic rate (RMR) calculation—*male*

1. Multiply your weight (pounds) by 6.3 _____ x 6.3 = _____
2. Multiply your height (inches) by 12.7 _____ x 12.7 = _____
3. Add 66 to the sum of Steps 1 and 2 _____ + 66 = _____
4. Multiply your age by 6.8 _____ x 6.8 = _____
5. Subtract Step 4 from Step 3 _____ − _____ = _____

RMR

Step 2   Active metabolic rate (AMR) calculation—*female* and *male*

To get your *AMR*, multiply your *RMR* from the calculation in Step 1 by the number that best describes your current level of physical activity (below). This indicates how many calories you can eat to maintain your weight without gain.

You have a desk job and don't exercise regularly: inactive = 1.2
You have a desk job but exercise or ride a few times a week: moderately active = 1.4
You have a physical job and exercise or ride a few times a week: very active = 1.6
You have a physical job and exercise or ride several times a day: extremely active = 1.8

Step 3   Weight loss goal

To calculate how many calories you need to ingest to safely lose weight, multiply your AMR from the calculation in Step 2 by the number below that best describes your current level of activity.

You have a desk job and don't exercise regularly: inactive = 0.79
You have a desk job but exercise or ride a few times a week: moderately active = 0.81
You have a physical job and exercise or ride a few times a week: very active = 0.83
You have a physical job and exercise or ride several times a day: extremely active = 0.85

2. Your body may "believe" you're trying to "starve" it. In response to this perceived threat, it will switch over to a *starvation-survival mode* by lowering its *RMR*, and because of the decreased demand for energy, your body will learn to burn fewer and fewer calories.

3. Much of the body weight you lose will be muscle mass. As you may recall, your muscles act like a metabolic furnace, burning lots of calories 24 hours a day. When you decrease your muscle mass through dieting, you also decrease the number of calories your body burns.

4. Less food enters your stomach. Your body will no longer need to burn as many calories to digest food.

Healthy Eating Tips

While horse show hamburgers and fries might smell great from across the show grounds, you need to avoid being tempted. Try these ten healthy eating tricks:

1. Instead of eating three large meals a day, take a lesson from your horse and try grazing. Eating several healthy "mini-meals" throughout the day helps you avoid becoming overly hungry and prone to "bingeing." It also helps keep your metabolism revved up by making your digestive system work all day. A nonfat yogurt and a piece of fruit are examples of healthy mini-meals.

2. Never underestimate the "power" of fat. Adding a little mayonnaise to your sandwich every day may not seem like a big deal, but over a year, these extra calories can add a pound of fat to your body—10 pounds in 10 years!

3. Always remember the 20-minute rule. It takes about 20 minutes for your body to recognize that it's full. If you eat too quickly, you outrace your body's *appetite control center.* Avoid this by slowing down your eating.

4. Keep a daily food diary by recording how many grams of fat, protein, carbohydrates, and calories you take in. You can find these totals on the nutrition labels of the foods you eat or in the nutrition content section of most healthy-eating books.

5. When eating in restaurants, place all the "fatty" appetizers—chicken-wings and creamy dips, for example—on the opposite side of the table. You can't eat what you can't reach.

6. Remember to order all toppings, oils, and sauces "on the side." Once they arrive, use them sparingly.

7. Instead of ordering food prepared with creamy sauces, select foods that use spices as their main source of flavoring.

8. Ask the waiter to divide your meal into two individual portions. Eat a half portion now and save the second half for a mini-meal later.

9. When you eat out, try to find a restaurant that has a salad bar. Be careful to avoid the salad ingredients like bacon bits and creamy dressings.

10. While waiting for your food to arrive, drink plenty of water. Filling your stomach may trick your body into feeling full, and no, this trick does not work with beer or margaritas!

PART FIVE

FRAME AND YOUR FRAME OF MIND

IN PREVIOUS CHAPTERS, YOU LEARNED HOW TO improve your mounted performance by refining your body's "frame." Now, you're going to learn how to improve your riding performance by refining your "frame of mind." This term is used to describe equestrian sport psychology and the important role it plays in achieving peak riding performance. Your ability to adapt to the stress and tension of riding, and the way you mentally approach your lessons or shows dictates how successful you'll be at achieving your riding goals. Improved performance, greater enjoyment, a sense of personal fulfillment, and a closer, more satisfying relationship with your horse, are a few of the benefits of a good frame of mind. I'm going to outline a variety of sport psychology techniques that can help you attain a heightened sense of mental focus, confidence, self-control, positive thinking, and patience. If used correctly, they can also help you overcome mental riding problems such as doubt, fear, stress, tension, and performance anxiety.

Your emotion controls your motion

A good mental attitude is important to your riding because your thoughts and feelings have a profound impact on your body's physical performance. To help you see how emotion and motion are so closely connected, simply imagine the posture of a worried rider. Her shoulders are rounded forward, muscles stiff and tight, and hands, head, fingers, and eyes fidgety. Now imagine the posture of a self-assured rider. Her shoulders are opened wide, head and eyes look forward with confidence, her muscles poised and ready to perform their best.

Improve your riding motion by learning to improve your riding emotion!

CHAPTER FOURTEEN

GOAL SETTING

Whether you realize it or not, you constantly set riding goals. You may do so on purpose or completely unintentionally. The problem with setting goals is that unless you do it correctly, you can become frustrated, disappointed, and lose motivation—three emotions that have no place in riding. You must first have a very clear idea of what it is you're trying to achieve. Once you've correctly identified your riding goals, you can set about achieving them with the help of the techniques in this section. Before you start, you should know that there are three different kinds of riding goals—two positive and one negative.

1. Behavioral Goals

These goals focus on your mental behavior on and around your horse. You can identify these

> *Have you ever wondered why your horse feels tense, nervous, unfocused, preoccupied, or distracted? Well, guess what... he might be wondering the same thing about you.*

goals by asking the question, "What traits do horses like their riders to have?" Considerate, patient, understanding, responsible, consistent, rewarding, kind, affectionate, knowledgeable, and caring are a few good answers. Listening to what your horse has to say, spending time with him outside your lessons, taking an active role in his health and soundness, and enjoying the time you spend with him are other good examples.

2. Performance Goals

These goals focus on working hard, doing your best, and feeling good about it. Riding a perfect 20 meter circle, nailing a difficult combination, remembering not to drop your shoulder in your turns, maintaining a positive attitude, and staying mentally focused are good examples of performance goals.

3. Outcome Goals

These goals focus on winning or beating one or more of your opponents. Winning three classes at a show or finishing in front of a rider who has beaten you in the past are *outcome goals*.

Unrealistic expectations, anxiety, poor performance, and disappointment are the result of a rider focusing on *outcome goals*. While we all prefer

Focus on the 1½ things you can control

Remember that you can control 100 percent of yourself. You can create a positive attitude by acting confidently and repeating positive affirmations to yourself. You can also control about half of your horse. You do this, not by using spurs, whips, or bits, but by making him more confident by being more confident, more supple by being more supple, and more balanced by being more balanced. You don't, however, have any control over the other riders, horses, or judges. So, your goals should not focus on any of these factors. Words such as, "I'll never reach my goal because his horse is more expensive than mine," or, "He beat me last week, my goal is to beat him this week," have no place in your goal vocabulary because you can only control one and a half things—you and your horse!

winning to losing (this trait is ingrained in most of our personalities), your goals should not focus on the result of an event but on the *process* required to achieve a desirable outcome. Imagine if you set an *outcome goal* of winning every class at a show, yet failed to win the very first class. In addition to feeling disappointed, you would lose much of the motivation needed to perform well in your remaining classes. If you are able to attain *behavioral* and *performance goals*, you'll probably succeed.

One problem that may arise when you are trying to attain your *performance* and *behavior goals* is that your horse might not feel like cooperating. He is, after all, a very unpredictable animal. He may do three perfect flying changes in a row, but buck his way through the fourth because a little bird has landed on a fence post. You should be prepared to quickly reevaluate, modify, or even completely change your goal, at this point.

Let's say your goal is to jump 8 fences cleanly, but your horse knocks over the first one. You can either feel disappointed, or remain positive by quickly reevaluating. Remember that you always have the choice to focus on

the negative or the positive. You original goal of jumping 8 good fences can be easily modified to jumping 7 fences cleanly, or even completely changed to a new goal of recovering well and finishing strong after a slow start. Being quick to react will ensure that you stay motivated and in positive "frame of mind."

Most people spend much more time schooling than showing. For this reason, you should set *performance* and *behavior goals* for your regular lessons and riding, not just your competitions. While there's nothing wrong with setting show goals if you ride competitively, achieving your schooling goals will actually ensure your success in the show ring.

When the difficulty of your goals *exceeds* your ability, disappointment usually ensues. When your ability is equal to, or greater than, the difficulty, the reverse is true and you are much more likely to succeed. Follow these six simple rules.

Goal-Setting Guidelines

1. Set positive goals. You always have the choice to focus on the positive or the negative. Remind yourself that you enjoy riding, like to be active, take pleasure in the company of your riding friends, and love your horse. I recall a rider in one of my clinics saying, "My goal is to ride well, but I'm too short and chubby." She forgot what she'd learned in a seminar I'd taught, that when you're short, you have a *low center of gravity*, and when you're chubby, you have a wide *base of support*—two attributes that lead to balance and stability. By the time she left, she learned to ignore her negative thoughts and replace them. She left the clinic saying (and believing), "My goal is to use my great balance to help me ride well." Overcome the tendency to focus on the negative by always phrasing your goals in a positive way. Removing negative words such as "not," "can't," and "won't" is all it takes to change a negative goal into a positive one. Don't say, "My goal is to *not* knock over a single jump today." Rephrase by simply saying, "My goal is to jump clear today." "I will not forget my course," can

"I'm going for the gold"

Does this statement describe an *outcome goal* or a *performance goal*? It's an *outcome goal* if you only focus on winning the gold, but a *performance goal* if you focus on the actual process required to win it—the "going for" part of the statement. The important part isn't the color of the medal but the way you act and perform when "going for it."

easily be replaced by, "I'm confident I will remember my course today." Since positive thinking is one of the basic principles of sport psychology, take the time to examine your riding goals and rephrase them.

2. *Make your goals measurable.* In order for you to know whether you've actually attained a goal, you need to be able to measure it. Learning the flying change is a good example because you know very easily when you've accomplished the goal.

3. *Develop achievement strategies.* Once you've set your performance and behavioral goals, establish strategies to help you achieve them. If your performance goal is to jump clear today, a good strategy is to make sure your approaches are straight, your pace and rhythm are good, your body position correct, and your eyes focused forward. Keeping your horse sound suggests reading a book on equine lameness, talking to your farrier about proper shoeing, and learning to apply a standing bandage to your horse's legs after a hard lesson.

4. *Record your goals.* It's easy to stay focused on your goals immediately after setting them. Wait a few months, however, and many will have become vague or even forgotten. Avoid this by writing your goals on a piece of paper and pinning it in a well-seen

spot—to your tack trunk or the post that holds your saddle. Once you've attained a goal, erase it, and substitute a new one.

5. *Reward yourself.* Each time you accomplish a goal, give yourself a little reward. A ten dollar bill and a tack store is one idea, though rewards don't need to be material.

The difference between a "win attitude" and a "winning attitude"

You have a *win attitude* if you only focus on winning. The path you take toward winning (doing your best and feeling good about doing your best) is not important to you. Beaten by other riders? Finish with anything less than a blue ribbon? You feel disappointed and upset with yourself.

You have a *winning attitude* when you take pride in working hard, listening to your horse and instructor, maintaining a positive attitude, learning from your mistakes, and remaining confident and happy in all riding situations—even when you don't perform well. Blaming your horse, other riders, or the judges never enters your mind.

Reach your goals by climbing a ladder

Imagine that your *long-term goal* is the top rung on a ladder and that you're standing on the ground. The first rung is your *immediate goal,* the remaining rungs are your *short-term goals.* The only way to get to the *long-term goal* is one rung at a time. The first step is the most important because it's the catalyst that gets you started in the right direction. Then work your way closer to the top by setting and achieving a series of short-term goals.

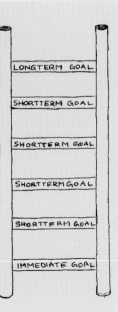

"One step at a time."

They can be something as simple as the pride you feel when you finally get to tell your best friend that you've accomplished something very meaningful to you.

6. *Share your goals with your riding peers.* When your friends know your goals, they can remind you when you forget. The encouragement and support they provide also helps to keep you motivated and focused.

Achieving a riding goal can be overwhelming. It's best to break it down into more manageable pieces. Your ultimate goal is your long-term goal, and it may take months or years to accomplish, and some may take for-ever. For instance, if you're a novice rider, a goal of learning to canter may take weeks or months, a goal of learning to jump may take months or years, and a goal of keeping your horse healthy will never end. Don't be afraid to set very long-term goals because when you work to achieve them you learn and improve as a horseperson.

Now that you're more familiar with goal-setting, take the time to think about your own riding goals. Once you've identified your most important performance and behavior goals, jot them down in your notebook or on Post-its. Set them up in a clear format as I've done below.

Goals

Date _____

Performance goal_____   Behavior goal _____

One immediate goal

1 _____

Three short-term goals

1 _____

2 _____

3 _____

One immediate goal

1 _____

Three short-term goals

1 _____

2 _____

3 _____

CHAPTER FIFTEEN

PEAK RIDING PERFORMANCE

In order to *Ride Right*, you must attain and maintain a state of peak physical and mental focus. When you accomplish this, your performance automatically, and without effort, will surpass your normal potential. This narrow window of concentration and focus is called *peak riding performance*, and often creates euphoria or a "natural high," which allows you to ride better than you ever thought possible. This "focused focus" is what's often called riding "in the zone." You feel as if your body moves perfectly without effort, your eyes looking forward but seeing everything in a peripheral manner. The sharp edges of your concentration are softened, and your eyes create an invisible bridge that joins your physical body and mental awareness.

The more physically fit and skilled a rider you are, the more control you have over your body. If you lack these two important attributes, you'll have a difficult time riding in the zone and an even more difficult time reaping the rewards and personal fulfillment created by riding at your full potential. The third attribute needed to achieve *peak riding performance* is *mounted awareness*. Positive thinking, concentration, visualization, relaxation, stress management, and mental focus all combine to create this.

Optimum Mounted Awareness

If you enter a competition or lesson with an apathetic attitude, your brain won't be able to convince your body to perform its best. Enter a competition or lesson with feelings of anxiety, and your body won't be able to convince your brain to perform its best. Your personality, riding discipline, and horse's disposition determine how physically and mentally aware you must be. (The stress management techniques mentioned later in this book have been designed to help you achieve *optimum mounted awareness.*)

Your Personality

Every rider in the world deals with competitive stress, performance anxiety, fear, and self-doubt in her own unique way. If you ride in an anxious, fearful, or tense manner, you must learn to lower your natural level of *mounted awareness* by using mental relaxation and confidence-building techniques. If you ride in an apathetic, unmotivated, burnt-out, depressed, uncaring, or lazy manner, or if you feel certain you're going to lose, you must increase your level of *mounted awareness* by using positive attitude, motivation, and self-confidence techniques. Regardless of your natural personality, sport psychology can help improve your riding by helping you remain aware, but never *anxious* or *apathetic.*

Signs of peak riding performance

Mentally and physically relaxed
Sense of time slowing down
Crystal clear concentration
Confident in challenging situations
Positive and optimistic
Highly energized
Sense of automatically doing "what's right"
Incredible body awareness
Feeling detached from all distractions
Effortless performance
Total immersion in riding
No feelings of fear or anxiety
Internal calmness
Feeling in complete control

Your Riding Discipline

Different riding disciplines require different levels of physical and mental awareness. Fast-paced equestrian sports that require frequent and quick changes of direction demand a high level of excitement. Polo, barrel racing, and show jumping are three examples of sports that require constant high awareness and stimulation. Disciplines that require suppleness and grace demand a different level of physical and mental awareness: dressage, equitation, and trail riding are examples where the emphasis is on being more physically and mentally *relaxed*, rather than charged-up. Some riding disciplines require both levels of awareness and stimulation. In endurance and competitive trail riding, you must be physically and mentally charged at the beginning and end, yet relaxed during the midsections to conserve your horse's energy. Three-day eventing is another such case because your level must be high during the cross-country and show jumping phases, yet more contained during the dressage portion.

Your Horse's Disposition

Your horse's personality also determines the amount of physical and mental awareness you must ride with. Even if you participate in show jumping, you'll need to ride with a lower level if your horse is "wild." The oppo-site holds true if you participate in dressage with a very unmotivated horse. Unless you can stimulate yourself, you won't be able to influence your horse.

Performance Anxiety and Fear

Here's a situation to ponder. You're a trainer (let's call you Mary) who is showing a student's horse. As you enter the ring, you overhear a trainer from your hometown call out to two other local trainers, "Hey guys, come over here so we can all watch Mary mess up!" Do you think this remark would cause you self-doubt, stress, and anxiety? If you're like most riders, the answer is probably yes. It could severely hinder your *performance potential* because it lowers your self-confidence, and then you feel that you're no longer in complete control. This is called *performance anxiety*, and you must learn to overcome it before it overcomes you.

Fear is also a factor in performance anxiety. There are two types of fear: fear of falling, and fear of failing. Unlike tennis and golf, riding—by the very nature of a horse's unpredictability—is a potentially frightening experience. Your tennis racket and golf club are always the same; they never get spooked, cranky, nervous, curious, afraid, or upset. A horse's aberrant behavior is not just limited to competition but can occur in any riding situation, from a trail ride to a lesson. Add your uncertainty to the speed, strength, power of the horse, plus your height off the ground, and it's easy to see how fear can arise.

Fear of failing, looking bad, performing poorly in front of others, letting down your trainer, disappointing your family, or not finishing as well as your peers are a few examples of fear of the outcome. These fears are usually, but not always associated with riding in a competitive atmosphere. Unfortunately, if these fears take over, it's difficult to avoid feeling *performance anxiety* and almost impossible to think in a confident manner and enjoy your ride.

Over the past 15 years, I've encountered riders who vomit, stop eating, break down and cry, or lose sleep before an important ride. I always ask myself, "What's so scary about riding or showing that causes these riders to experience such severe physical responses?" After all, aren't these the kind of reactions we usually associate with devastating events, such as losing a job or learning that a friend has unexpectedly passed away?

Performance anxiety usually arises from the same basic cause: a perceived loss of control. When you feel in control, you feel confident and self-assured, but when you feel that you've lost control, you are anxious and maybe fearful, too. When these emotions are powerful enough to evoke a physical change in your body, the response is said to be *psychosomatic* in nature (see Sidebar, below). Think back to when you had to take an important exam at school. Do you remember how your hands began sweating just before entering the exam room? Perhaps your stomach became upset (as mine often did before a show when I was a young rider) or you started yawning more than normal.

Stress Management Techniques

There are many proven ways to overcome *performance anxiety*, but for them to be successful, you must first identify the situations that cause you stress. You can then choose any of the following *stress management techniques* to help overcome your fear or psychosomatic symptoms.

1. Riding rehearsal. Prior to riding, find a quiet location, relax, close your eyes, and rehearse in your mind how your ride will look. For instance, you can visualize jumping a course by approaching each fence with perfect rhythm and straightness, bending in a supple manner around each corner, and jumping in balance over every fence. Make your visualizations as close to the real thing as possible by feeling things such as the sun on your shoulders and hearing sound of your horse's hooves.

Whenever possible, your rehearsal should last the exact same amount of time as the ride

you are about to do. If your event takes too long—a long cross-country course, or a hundred-mile endurance race—*imagine* the key points of your ride. Try to complete 3 perfect mental rehearsals before you even mount. When you do this, you'll have a big advantage over the other riders because you've already ridden your ride 3 times before! If someone interrupts you while you are visualizing your ride, politely say that you're in the middle of riding and will talk once you're finished.

2. Simulation training. This technique is similar to the *riding rehearsal*, only instead of visualizing your ride going perfectly, imagine a few of the things that can go wrong and how you are going to feel about it. Let's say you're competing in front of a large crowd (producing *performance anxiety*), when you see a dog playfully looking at your horse (making you *uncertain*), and you hear the motor of a tractor backfire beside you (*frightening*). Simulate each situation in your mind, and imagine handling it perfectly by smiling at the crowd, giving the dog your best "don't you dare," look and taking a deep breath

The best riding rehearsal of all

Try this simple trick to help make your riding rehearsals as vivid as possible. Stand on your Stable Board and actually ride the course as you visualize it. For example, if you're thinking about riding balanced around your corners, actually do a turn on your board that mimics the turn you're doing in your mind. Joining your mental and physical skills in this manner is one of the best ways to ensure that both your mind and body will benefit from the riding rehearsal.

after the tractor noise. By doing this, you learn how to identify and cope with stressful situations, regain control over them, and take pride in your ability to ride confidently.

3. *Systemic desensitization.* This technique is similar to *simulation training*, only instead of using it just prior to riding or competing, you use it during your lessons. It's particularly effective when trying to overcome a serious, stress-inducing problem because you learn the mental tools needed to handle it in the comfort and safety of your regular lesson, even if it's not present there. *Imagine* that you encounter the stressful event, and recreate the exact same physical and emotional feelings that occur during the real event. For instance, imagine your heart beginning to pound, your breathing becoming shallow and rapid, and your hands tightening around your reins. You can also ask your instructor to help you feel this atmosphere by vividly describing the stress-inducing event, as well as the symptoms you have often felt.

Once you're able to recall these feelings, slowly start to relax your body, even though you're still visualizing the stressful event. Concentrate on one body part at a time, and soon, you'll be able to completely relax. Then, replace the *imagined* event with the *real* one, and use the same techniques to help you relax and regain control. First duplicate, then eliminate tension, fear, and uncertainty, and your mind will become desensitized to the stress of the actual event.

4. *Memory motivation.* Relax deeply prior to competing or riding and recall the very best ride of your life. Recapture the feelings of ease, flow, mastery, and joy that you felt during that great ride and place them onto your upcoming ride. You can even plug these wonderful emotions into your *riding rehearsal.*

5. *Imagery relaxation.* This stress management technique is also called *detachment* because you're encouraged to mentally remove yourself from a stressful situation and imagine that you're in a pleasant, stress-free place. The location can be a "dream," like floating gently on a sailboat in a warm summer breeze or drinking margaritas on a Caribbean beach, or it can be your real favorite place, like inside your horse's stall or lying in front of your fireplace. One student even told me that her "quiet space" was at her favorite donut shop! My favorite place is swimming in the ocean with my mare and surfing when a wave lifts her and floats her

Mental practice makes perfect

Mentally rehearsing a skill prior to riding can have a profound effect on your mounted performance because it generates the same nerve responses in your muscles and brain. In other words, your body can't differentiate between an *imagined* practice and a *real* one. If done correctly, every time you visualize yourself riding, your body will believe you're actually doing so. This is called the "psychoneuromuscular theory," and it states that unmounted imagery sessions can be every bit as beneficial to your riding as your actual mounted sessions.

toward the shore. Regardless of the location you choose, *imagery relaxation* works best when you use as many of your five senses as possible. Try to hear the sounds of the waves, feel the warmth of the sand beneath your feet, see the fire as it burns in the fireplace, smell the freshness of the ocean breeze, and imagine the sweet taste of the donuts. This technique is very effective at lessening the stress of a riding situation because it removes you from it all together.

6. *Positive brain babble.* The words you say to yourself greatly influence your riding behavior. I call internal dialogue (or self-talk) *brain babble*, because your inner voice doesn't seem to know how to turn itself off. It just keeps babbling on. When your *brain babble* is negative, you limit your chances of riding well because you are convincing yourself otherwise. If you continually repeat, "I won't ride well today because everyone is better than I am," you've already convinced yourself you don't stand a chance.

When your *brain babble* is positive it does just the opposite. Imagine how much better you might ride after repeating, "I feel great, confident, and in control!" a few times. Since eliminating *negative brain babble* and changing it to *positive brain babble* has such a positive effect on your performance and enjoyment, I'm going to talk more about it in the next chapter (p. 153).

7. *Self-directed relaxation.* Relaxing your muscles deeply before riding or competing can

Ride as if it's your very first time on a horse

If the stress of riding is getting the best of you, think back to how it felt when you rode for the very first time. You probably felt thrilled and excited to be on top of this big, four-legged animal. Your riding goals were more about having fun, being active, spending time outdoors, and bonding with your horse than winning ribbons, jumping fences, and competing in front of big crowds. It's normal to challenge yourself throughout your riding career by setting new goals, but when these goals cause you stress, take a few deep breaths, relax, think positive thoughts, imagine yourself riding well, and recall all the wonderful emotions you felt when you rode for the very first time.

have an equally relaxing effect on your mind, as well. To perform this technique, also known as *progressive relaxation*, contract one group of muscles for 5 seconds, and then let it relax. The principle behind *self-directed relaxation* is that muscles achieve a deeper state of relaxation immediately following a contraction.

Start by contracting the muscles of your forehead (feel as the furrows deepen), and then relax so they disappear. Next, contract and relax your face muscles, followed by your shoulders, arms, hands, chest, and so on down. Move through your body until you've contracted and relaxed every muscle. Your mind and body will feel completely relaxed.

8. *Put it all together with deep breathing.* Every time you feel riding-related anxiety, take a deep breath and exhale. Better yet, spend a few minutes relaxing your body and focusing your mind by taking many deep breaths. At first, feel your body tense slightly with each inhalation and deeply relax with each exhalation. After a few deep breaths, feel your body relax after both the inhalation and exhalation. Each time you do, your blood will become richly oxygenated helping your mind sharpen and your muscles strengthen. While breathing calmly, repeat positive *brain babble*, recall your best ride ever (*memory motivation*),

Convince yourself that stressful situations aren't so bad by unleashing the power of your smile. To feel this power, close your eyes and think of a bad time. Frown and hunch your shoulders forward. Really try to feel the situation and the stress it causes you. After 15 seconds, open your shoulders confidently and "turn your frown upside down" with the biggest, brightest, smile possible. You can even let out a little giggle while you're at it.

Continue to think of this situation. How does it feel now? If you are like most people, you'll likely feel more confident, relaxed, and in control than before.

practice your *self-directed relaxation*, or enact your *riding rehearsal* a few times.

The goal of all these techniques is to help you reach a perfect level of *mental* and *physical awareness*, not make you so relaxed that you become a "gooey" blob in the saddle! Don't forget that you must feel some degree of stimulation to ride well. It should feel like a good case of the "butterflies," or "I-can't-wait excitement," but not like a case of uncontrollable dread or apathy.

Concentration

Stress management techniques are only effective when you're able to focus. When other stressful thoughts or external interruptions occur while you are trying to overcome a riding problem, they make it impossible for you to relax and achieve *optimum mounted awareness*. The only way to overcome the challenges is to block out everything else happening in your life and concentrate *completely* on your riding.

If you've ever ridden while thinking about a bothersome problem at work, or spent a lesson joking with the other riders, you probably noticed that you weren't able to ride your best. I remember teaching a very accomplished rider who, after taking a phone call from his office, could no longer figure out how to tell which trot diagonal he was on.

Twenty minutes before the end of the lesson, he felt so frustrated and unable to cope, he had to dismount and end the day.

Many people live a very hectic life, juggling issues of family, work, school, and money. You must learn, however, to set these aside to fully focus on the task of riding, until you dismount. Your horse is too much of a "clairvoyant" to let you get away with anything less than 100 percent concentration. He knows when you're thinking about him, or when you're thinking about something else. When you don't give him 100 percent of yourself, you can't expect him to give you 100 percent of himself. Remember, he doesn't care if you're being audited, studying for a big exam, or in the middle of a big account at work. He only cares that you dedicate all of your physical and mental efforts to him and your lesson. After all, you don't want him thinking of mares or oats during your lesson, so why should he expect anything less from you!

One unique technique that can help you *refocus* your concentration after a momentary

Not all stress is bad. In fact, some stress is actually better than no stress at all. In order to improve as a rider, you must expose yourself to challenging situations. The resulting stress you experience is called "eustress," and when you face and overcome it, you strengthen your self-confidence and grow as a rider.

While *eustress* is good for your development, a second kind of stress—*distress*—is harmful to your growth. It creates feelings of fear, loss of control, and the consequent psychosomatic responses. *Distress* causes your body to sweat or your hands to shake. Your job as a rider is to increase the amount of *eustress* in your riding and eliminate the *distress*.

lapse is called a *concentration cue*. This can be a noise, specific location, or physical movement of your body. For instance, you can decide that the *sound* of the bell ringing before you ride a dressage test, or the "Good luck," from your instructor, will be the cue to redirect your attention. Likewise, you can decide that a *location*, such as the gate you go through into the arena to start a jumping class, or passing specific route markers in an endurance race, will be used as your cue to refocus your concentration. Perhaps the most unusual, but also the most effective *concentration cues* are those

that use a physical movement of your body. As an example, if you feel self-doubt, remind yourself to feel more positive by manipulating your hands to give yourself two-thumbs-up. (I list several other physical *concentration cues* in the sidebar below.)

Always respect the *cue* by immediately refocusing your attention on your riding. If the cue doesn't work, find another one, or try one from another category. Above all, remember that riding is your passion, so don't let the other stresses in your life take the joy away from it or hinder your performance.

Concentration cues

The best physical *concentration cues* are those that can be done while mounted and without removing your hands from the reins.

1. Stop thinking about work by moving your hands to mimic slamming your office door.

2. Stop thinking about an argument with a friend by moving your hand to imitate hanging up the phone. Call her back when you've finished riding.

3. Make light of stressful riding situations by shrugging your shoulders as if to say, "Hey, no big deal."

4. Stop worrying about falling off by fastening an imaginary seatbelt securely around your waist.

5. See everything in a new way by simply shutting your eyes for a moment and opening them to a more positive environment.

6. Stop thinking about school and imitate closing a book.

7. Use a few deep breaths as your *concentration cue* to relax and think confidently.

CHAPTER SIXTEEN

BRAIN BABBLE

While on a teaching trip in Gladstone, New Jersey, I noticed a homeless man sitting on a bench engaged in what appeared to be a deep conversation with himself. Upon closer examination, I noticed that while he was certainly talking to himself, he was actually sharing his conversation with a picture of an attractive female newscaster painted on the bench. As a rider, you can learn something very useful from this man and that's the ability to carry on a positive and meaningful conversation with yourself, even without a photo to talk to!

Brain babble, or the words you "think" to yourself, has a major affect on your ability to remain confident in the saddle. Positive thoughts and affirmations help you stay self-assured, feel more enjoyment, and take greater control of your riding experiences. Negative thoughts, on the other hand, create feelings of self-doubt, dread, inability to cope, or hopelessness. You

> *Fake it until you make it!*
> *When you feel uncertain or nervous, continually repeat to yourself that you're confident and in total control. Don't stop this until you actually feel confident and in total control.*

have the choice to focus on the positive or negative.

An older rider I teach used to tell herself that she wouldn't do well at shows because of her age. Now, she tells herself she's going to do "great" because of her wealth of knowledge, her disciplinary habits, and her experience. She now enjoys competing more than ever, having once again found the thrill and delight she used to feel. She's overcome her

Negative brain babble

Originating from every aspect of your riding, *negative brain babble* has a profound affect on your riding performance and enjoyment. Your horse's physical abilities, your body and emotional state, and of course, opponents in competition, can all cause you to think in a negative manner. For example:

"All the other riders are better than me."

"Darn, Mary's competing today, so I might as well not even ride."

"I'm going to lose because my horse is stiffer, (smaller), (greener), (less expensive) than the others."

"I don't stand a chance because I'm a bad rider."

"I jump horribly because I always look down."

"I'm too overweight to ride well."

"I look stupid on my horse because my legs are too short."

"I get so nervous riding in front of strangers."

"Riding on windy days makes me scared."

Recognizing where your negative thoughts come from is the first step to reforming them.

toughest opponent—not the younger competitor—but her own negative brain babble.

You often don't know you're thinking in a negative way until it's too late. It simply creeps its way into your psyche—uninvited. Learn to block these thoughts from your mind before they arrive by recognizing the situations that cause them so you can remind yourself in advance to think positively. In the event that negative thoughts *do* enter your mind, a simple mental technique called *thought-stopping* can help you disrupt them. "Yell" a word, such as "stop," "whoa," or "hey" to yourself. You disrupt the flow of negativity, and get back to positive thinking.

Using a thought-stopper

Negative brain babble
"I blew my first 10 meter circle, my half-pass was horrible, the judge hates me, I might as well quit."

Thought-stopper
"I blew my first 10 meter circle, my half-pass was horrible, the judge…Whoa!…I'm confident in my ability to finish well after a slow start, and the remaining skills required are easy for me."

Brain Babble Guidelines

1. Avoid negative words. Words like "can't," "won't," and "no," are unmistakably negative, but others aren't so obvious. In fact, many words that normally have a positive connotation become quite negative. When you use the words "try," "hope," and "think," you imply a degree of uncertainty or self-doubt. The confident statement, "I *know* I can do it," becomes instead, "I *think* I can do it," "I'll *try* and do it," or "I *hope* I can do it." All these imply less than 100 percent self-confidence.

2. Leave out the negative. Because your brain doesn't recognize the word "not," you need to phrase your statements in a positive way. "I'm confident I'll make all of my flying changes today," is much better than saying, "I'm confident I *won't* miss any of my flying

changes today." Say, "I'm relaxed and focused," instead of "I will *not* get tense and lose my focus." Take the phrase, "Do not think of a carrot." If you're like most people, you immediately thought about a carrot even though you were clearly instructed not to. Your brain didn't recognize the word "not," simply registering, "*Do* think of a carrot." Similarly, "I will not tense up, and I will not lose my focus," becomes, "I will tense up, and I will lose my focus."

3. Make your positive brain babble memorable. When your thoughts are funny or foolish, you have a better chance of remembering them. If you get nervous riding in front of strangers, think to yourself, "I love riding in front of people," or, "Hey everyone, get out your cameras because this is going to be a Kodak moment you're not going to want to miss!" And, nothing is better for releasing stress and tension than a little laughter.

4. Avoid "trash-talkers." These people only see the negative. They approach you, and can, in the span of ten seconds, dump a whole load of "mental trash" at your feet. "It rained the other day, so the footing's going to be horrible." "The judge is mean." "I hate it when it's windy." "You must be so nervous, how can you handle the pressure?" All are examples of this kind of trash. To avoid being weighed down, you must "slam the lid on them" with a positive response. "Hey, you're right, it did

A positive attitude is a balancing act

If you've repeated a negative statement 100 hundred times, you need to repeat the positive, replacement statement at least 101 times before you can tilt the balance of positive thinking in your favor. In fact, some studies show that for every negative statement you make, you need to repeat its positive opposite 35 times before you begin to believe it. That's the power of negative thinking!

rain the other day so that means it won't be dusty." "I'm glad the judge is critical because she can help me learn what I need to work on in the future." "I love the wind because it helps me stay fresh and cool." "Thanks for reminding me of all these great things, I really feel confident about my riding now!" The "trash-talker" will realize she is no match for you, and will take her mental garbage elsewhere. Remember, you don't take garbage from a real trash can so you shouldn't take it from a "trash-talker" either!

5. *When all else fails, think of the letter C.* This isn't some kind of spelling test but an easy way to help you come up with *positive brain babble.* The next time you start to think in a negative way, yell a *thought-stopper,* and think of all positive words that begin with C. Calm, cool, collected, courageous, confident, centered, competent, capable, carefree, committed, composed, controlled, and can, are a few good examples. Next time you need to remind yourself what a great rider you are, repeat a couple of these great "C" words to yourself.

6. *Place an emphasis on each word in your positive phrase.* Once you've come up with a positive statement, repeat it to yourself several times when confronted with a challenging situation. Instead of repeating it in a normal manner, however, place an emphasis on the first word of the sentence the first time you say it. The second time, place the emphasis on the second word, and so on, until you've placed the emphasis on every single word in the sentence. By the time you finish, you'll actually believe what you've just said to yourself. You might just chuckle to yourself a little as you realize the silliness of this technique, but this is good thing because, as I mentioned before, nothing can help you rid yourself of stress better than a little giggle.

The Four R's

Learn to change *negative brain babble* into *positive brain babble* by completing your Four R's:

Recall riding situations that you think about in a negative way.

Rank them from *least* to *most* stressful, and write down what you thought during each event. Start with the least stressful event, and…

Replace the negative thought with a positive thought, and visualize it helping you to relax, derive pleasure from, and regain control of that event.

Record the new *positive brain babble* by crossing the old negative thought off your list and writing down the new positive statement. Once you've dealt with the least stressful event, move to the next one on your list and deal with it, too. Soon, *positive brain babble* will make you feel relaxed, confident, and in control of all your previously stressful riding events. Think about these positive thoughts each time you encounter similar situations in the future.

CHAPTER SEVENTEEN

VISUALIZATION AND MENTAL IMAGERY

Your brain is made up of two unique halves called *hemispheres*, and each is responsible for a variety of important tasks (fig. 17.1). The *left hemisphere* (often called the *analyzer*) makes tasks such as language, sequential planning, logic, computation, and self-instruction possible. This is the portion of your brain that permits you to create *brain babble*, set riding *goals*, learn new skills (by reading), correct flaws in your technique, and develop strategies. When this hemisphere is in control, your attention is usually focused on learning from past performances or planning for future ones.

The *right hemisphere* is where your ability to think creatively, move purposefully and effortlessly, orient yourself in space, and use mental images originates. While much of your riding-skill acquisition occurs in the *left hemisphere*, your *right brain* (often called the *inte-*

grator) integrates the many clumsy *left-brain* components of a newly learned skill into one simple flowing image. The most effective way to train your *right brain* is to continually create little mental pictures in your mind. Unlike the *left hemisphere* that focuses on the past and future, your attention is usually focused on the present when you use your *right hemisphere* while riding.

In order for *images* to be successful, they must be vivid and lifelike. You accomplish this by using as many of your senses as you can when you visualize. Try to feel, smell, hear, taste, and see each *image* as if it was real, and your mind can easily solve problems your body has tried to correct unsuccessfully for years.

A dressage rider attending one of my clinics learned very quickly how *imagery* solves long-lasting physical problems. She told me that she'd like to improve the suppleness of her arms so that she no longer squeezed her elbows into her ribs. Since she's a dressage rider, we both agreed she should learn to relax her arms and carry her elbows a small distance away from her sides. To accomplish this, I asked her to *imagine* wearing a pair of children's water wings on her arms. Suddenly, to my surprise, the organizer of the clinic, which was being held in the community center of an equestrian facility, ran out to the pool deck and returned with an actual pair of children's plastic water wings. To the rider's dismay, I had her put them on while standing in front of 40 strangers and asked her to feel them pressing against her skin, smell the chlorine on the plastic,

17.1 Brain Hemispheres

Left Hemisphere	Right Hemisphere
Setting goals	Visualization
Correct flaws in technique	Body awareness
Learning a skill for first time	Effortless performance
Self-instruction (brain babble)	Confidence and other emotions
Reading equestrian books	Mental rehearsal
Develop riding strategies	Internal calmness
Memorizing courses	Mental focus

You need your entire brain to Ride Right. Both left and right brain areas are responsible for numerous, important riding tasks.

and see the bright blue and pink design. Being a kind person, I didn't ask her to use her sense of taste and lick the water wings! However, I did want her to use her sense of hearing, so noticing that the wings were over-inflated, which caused her arms to lie too far away from her body, I uncorked the air valves and asked her to relax her arms. As she did, a little air escaped, and a low hissing sound came out from the valves. We'd done it! We'd found sound! Since she was able to use four of her five senses, the visualization became so real that she was able to correct her physical problem, not by using her body but by using her mind. Today, all she needs to do is imagine this rather foolish, yet vivid image, and she relaxes her arms, and they float away from her sides.

Mental images can be *external* or *internal*. *External imagery* is used when you visualize yourself, or another rider, through the lens of a video camera or by looking down from above, like from a helicopter. This technique gives you the "big picture" of a riding skill: remember a jumping course or mentally rehearse a dressage test before attempting it, for instance.

Internal imagery is used to develop a "feeling" inside your body that helps you perfect a riding movement—see the example mentioned before of the rider relaxing and opening her arms by visualizing that she's wearing a pair of children's water wings. In general, *internal imagery* is most helpful when you are actually riding.

Mental Imagery Guidelines

1. Relax. Mental *images*, including *stress management techniques* like *riding rehearsals*, *simulation training*, and *memory motivation* are most effective when done in a calm atmosphere with no distractions. To maximize their effectiveness, perform them while breathing deeply, or when practicing *self-directed relax-*ation. When using *imagery* while riding or during difficult situations using *systemic desensitization* and *detachment*, try your best to relax, and breathe deeply.

2. Grab something. Help your mind understand your visualizations by "feeling" the actual item you plan on using for your mental *images*. For instance, you can develop good

Left brain and right brain

When you learn a new skill, you use the *left* side of your brain to list the things to do—you *analyze* the skill. Once you can perform the skill, the *right brain integrates* the list into one flowing image.

The canter depart is a good example of how this can work. When you learn the canter depart, you likely repeat a list something like, "inside leg at the girth, outside leg back, inside rein open, outside rein snug." Once cantering becomes second nature to you, however, you probably stop repeating the phrase, and simply place your hands, feet, and body where they need to be. Your *left brain* no longer needs to analyze the list because your *right brain* has taken over and integrated it into a single image.

rein tension by imagining you're holding a small sponge in each hand and slowly squeezing a drop of warm water out of each one. This image will become clearer in your mind if you actually grab two small sponges, place one in each hand, and gently squeeze a few warm drops of water out of them. The next time you ride, recall how the warm sponges felt in your hands and the amount of tension you needed to squeeze out the drops of water. If you practice this while riding, and I suggest you do, you'll know when your hands are in a good position because the drops of water will land on each side of your horse's neck.

3. Use a movement bridge. Make your mental *images* more effective by performing a physical movement to get the visualization underway. When you do this, the movement

Daydreaming is good for your riding

When control switches smoothly from one side of the brain to the other, your *analyzer*—the *left* side—corrects riding errors and develops strategies, while your *integrator*—the *right* side—integrates the skills in a fluid and automatic motion. Unfortunately, this cooperation often turns into a competition. When your *analyzer* wins the quest for control, which often happens, you over-analyze a skill, and it becomes mechanical without the *right* brain's *integrating* it into one motion. Now, it's impossible to ride in a graceful manner.

One reason the left brain wins its battle against the right brain is because society places more importance on learning logic than imagery. Parents and teachers constantly reward youngsters for thinking logically, yet punish them for daydreaming. In addition, many schools with budget concerns are eliminating right brain activities, such as art and music. By the time most students graduate, they've learned to suppress their right brain and overuse their left.

becomes a *bridge* between the image and the skill you're trying to accomplish. You can learn to ride with your eyes focused forward by pretending it's nighttime, and you're riding with a small miner's light attached to your helmet. It's dark out, so you must always look forward and follow the light shining between your horse's ears. To create the *movement bridge* between your mind and body, actually reach up with one hand and imitate the motion of turning on the switch of your make-believe miner's light. This kind of movement will remind you to use your images, as well as strengthen their effect.

4. Make your visualizations memorable. You'll have an easier time remembering your mental *images* if they're foolish or funny. For instance, an instructor once tried to help me develop independent hands by asking me to hold an imaginary bowl of hot soup while I was riding. I liked this image, but the thought of spilling steaming hot soup all over my horse made me tense. A few years later, another instructor tried to accomplish the same thing by asking me to hold an imaginary tray of margaritas and martinis. What made it even sillier was that he said it was his "liquid lunch" and that I had better not spill a drop. As I was visualizing the image, he encouraged me to "see" the yellow color of the margaritas, the salt on the rim of the glasses, the olives in the martinis, and the napkins on the tray. Almost immediately, I started riding with more supple and independent hands. While the bowl of soup may work for some people, the image of holding my instructor's liquid lunch seemed so weird and foolish that I never forgot it!

A ballerina vs. an accountant

An accountant works with numbers and logic and develops a strong *left brain*. A ballerina works with grace, rhythm, and imagery and develops a strong *right brain*. If you leased your horse to a stranger and had to choose an accountant or a ballerina, who do you think you'd prefer? While there are hundreds of great accountant riders, you'd probably still choose the ballerina because her right-brain training has taught her how to move in a supple and graceful manner.

5. *Pretend to be someone else.* Use *external imagery* to visualize a rider you admire. Perhaps she has a perfect leg, great posture, supple hands, wonderful rhythm, or amazing confidence. The next time you ride, imagine stealing her legs, posture, hands, rhythm, and confidence, and make them your own. Repeat to yourself, "I'm riding with Mary's legs, posture, hands, rhythm, and confidence!" You'll be amazed at how well this *identity-swapping* trick works. Another way *identity swapping* can help your performance is to imagine being the designer who sets up a jumping course. Instead of fearing you're going to forget the course, repeat to yourself, "I'm confident I can remember the course because I'm the one who designed it." As you repeat the words, imagine how you placed the flowers in their pots, spaced the jumps just so, raised and lowered the heights, and drew the final diagram.

6. *Watch yourself.* Help develop your mind's eye by watching yourself ride in mirrors, or look at photographs or videotape. Concentrate on looking for your riding strengths, remember them as an image, and recall them the next time you are uncertain about your riding.

7. *Tell others.* Sharing your mental *images* enables your riding peers and instructors to remind you to use them whenever you forget. For instance, if you use the image of a miner's light to keep your eyes focused forward, your instructor can ask you if your batteries are dead every time you look down.

Examples of Mental Images

Following is a brief list of images for riders. While I've tried to provide at least one image for each body part, you still might not find the one that's perfect for you. Not all images work for everyone, use the guidelines provided on the previous pages, and come up with a few of your own.

- Release tension in your head by imagining your cheeks are sagging like a bloodhound's, or you have triple chins like a turkey.

- Relax your mouth (tension here travels to your neck and shoulders) by opening it slightly and imagining a fly just flew in. Hear the fly buzzing around in your mouth, and keep it open slightly so that he can fly out.

- Keep your eyes focused forward by imagining that you're looking at (and seeing) the exact same thing as your horse.

- Breathe rhythmically while riding by imagining that you have a trick birthday candle in front of your face, and you are continually blowing it out as it relights itself.

- Open your shoulders by imagining someone is lengthening the back of your neck by pulling upward on your ponytail.

- Or, open your shoulders by imagining you're riding on a windy day, and the howling wind is blowing your shoulders open. To make this image more visual, stick your hand out of the window of your car the next time you drive down the highway. Remember this sensation and imagine this wind pushing your shoulders back.

Mental imagery can help you:

- Rehearse a skill
- Avoid riding problems in the future by solving them in the present
- Overcome situations that cause you anxiety or stress
- Memorize the order of complicated skills or movements
- Recall mistakes so you don't repeat them in the future
- Relax and concentrate
- Learn skills by visualizing yourself or someone else doing them

- Sit up tall by imagining you are standing guard outside Buckingham Palace.

- Perfect your posture by imagining you are riding with a stack of books on your head.

- Keep your hips facing forward by imagining a small laser beam coming out of your belly button and shining between your horse's ears. If you twist to one side, the laser beam will slice all the hair off his ear.

- Develop good hip movement when posting the trot by imagining your lower torso is actually the hind leg of your horse.

- Develop supple hips while sitting the trot by imagining that the cheeks of your buttocks are large beach balls with half the air let out of them. If the balls are completely full of air, they become tight and tense, which causes them to bounce or rebound upward when dropped on the ground. Since your balls are only half full of air, they are not hard, don't bounce or rebound upward, and stay still and supple in the saddle.

- Develop a good canter motion by imagining your hips are doing a front-and-back hula-hoop motion or scooping ice cream out of a bucket, and your britches are polishing your saddle each time your hips move forward.

- Hold the reins with the correct amount of tension by imagining you are holding a small wet sponge in each hand and slowly squeezing a drop of warm water out of each one as you close your fingers.

- Keep your arms supple by imagining you are holding a bowl of warm soup or a tray of colorful drinks. Don't spill!

- Develop a good following hand by imagining your forearms are the forward-and-backward-moving metal arms that drive the wheels of an old-fashioned train.

- Stop yourself from riding too far forward by imagining a cartoon-like porcupine on your horse's withers saying, "I wouldn't do that if I were you." Avoid using more scary images, such as a row of metal spikes, because they could cause you to become tense.

Mental imagery is like a fortune-teller

Like a fortune-teller or a palm reader, *mental imagery* helps you "see into the future" by visualizing the kinds of riding problems you'll likely experience. When they arrive, you'll be more prepared to handle them because you've already encountered them, even if it was only in your mind.

- Imagine you have a pair of car keys in your back pocket and when you ride too far back, you will feel them digging into your buttocks.

- Place equal weight in both seat bones and stirrups by imagining you have a hundred-dollar bill under each seat bone and on top of each stirrup iron. If you place more weight on one side, the money on the opposite side flies away into the hands of your instructor, who then keeps it!

Riding is about choice and control

The amount of comfort, enjoyment, and success you achieve is dependent upon *choice* and *control*. You have the choice to control uncertain or anxiety-making riding situations, or you have the choice to let these situations control you. Learn to take a solid hold of the reins and steer yourself in the direction of confident riding by becoming more focused, self-assured, positive, and goal-oriented.

- Stop pinching your knees by imagining you're sitting on a speeding motorcycle, and the wind is forcing your knees open (again, sticking your hand out of the car window will help you feel how the wind can push you backward).

- Wrap your legs around your horse by imagining they're the gooey, gray tentacles of an octopus. Hear the suction cups going "phup-phup-phup" as your tentacle-like legs suck on and wrap all the way around and under the belly of your horse.

- Keep your heels down by imagining your toes are trying to touch your knees, and your calves are the shock absorbers on a car.

- Relax and spread your toes by imagining warm water running down your legs and trickling between your toes.

Fill in the blanks

Copy this page and write down 3 mounted problems that have always bothered you:

1 _____

2 _____

3 _____

Now write down 3 images that can help solve these problems:

1 _____

2 _____

3 _____

Keep it close to your tack trunk or saddle so that you're reminded of your images each time you ride.

CHAPTER EIGHTEEN

BEHAVIOR
INVENTORY TEST

I developed the *behavior inventory test* (*BIT*) to help you identify your mental strengths and weaknesses. It's easy to take, and there's no studying required. You can write in this book, photocopy the pages, or jot all the answers down in a separate notebook.

To take the test, which is in three sections, complete the underlined statements, and pick the adverbs that best describe *your* responses. Make a separate list of the statements that you responded to with "never," and add to it: one *positive brain babble* statement, one *immediate goal*, and two *short-term goals* (see *Brain Babble*, p. 153 and *Goal Setting*, p. 141). This will be your program to work on. Put the list beside your saddle or tack trunk so that you can refer to the *brain babble* and *goals* before every ride.

Work on your "never" responses in Section One for one week by repeating your *positive brain babble* statements, and following your *goals*. By the end of the first week, you should be able to move your responses from the "never" column to the "always" or "often" column.

During the second and third weeks, repeat this procedure for the "never" answered statements in Sections Two and Three. In weeks four, five, and six write *positive brain babble* statements and *goals* that change all "rarely" responses to "often" or "always." Weeks seven, eight, and nine should be dedicated to changing all the "occasional" answers to "often" or "always."

Retake the test to see if any answers have crept their way back into the "occasionally," "rarely," or "never," category and repeat the above steps, if necessary. If you feel that a week isn't enough time to work through each section, take longer.

Solve stressful riding situations

Describe a scenario where you feel frightened, stressed, or unable to cope: _____

Take control of this situation by writing down one:

Positive brain babble _____

Image _____

Goal _____

End by choosing the stress management technique(s) you think will best solve the problem, and invent a concentration cue to help you stay focused.

Stress management technique _____

Concentration cue _____

Photocopy this page and place it near your tack trunk or saddle so that you can read it each time you ride.

I'm aware this test creates some homework. However, it will be worth the time and effort— you'll be rewarded with a more positive, self-confident, and "in control" attitude. You never stop learning, so don't cheat yourself out of the benefits that a *long-term* program can provide. Remind yourself of how important each statement is to the success of your riding and to your life with horses.

Ask your instructor or riding peers to take this test, but instead of filling it out for themselves, ask them to rate *you*. Compare your responses with theirs. Discuss any differences, find out why they exist, and work together on how to solve them.

Section One – Goal Setting

always	often	I set performance goals	occasionally	rarely	never
always	often	I set behavior goals	occasionally	rarely	never
always	often	I focus on my performance—not on winning	occasionally	rarely	never
always	often	I set goals for showing	occasionally	rarely	never
always	often	I set goals for schooling	occasionally	rarely	never
always	often	I set attainable goals	occasionally	rarely	never
always	often	I create goal strategies	occasionally	rarely	never
always	often	I set immediate goals	occasionally	rarely	never
always	often	I set short-term goals	occasionally	rarely	never
always	often	I set long-term goals	occasionally	rarely	never
always	often	I record my goals	occasionally	rarely	never
always	often	I tell my goals to others	occasionally	rarely	never
always	often	I reward myself for attaining goals	occasionally	rarely	never
always	often	I value learning from my mistakes	occasionally	rarely	never
always	often	I set goals that are easily modifiable	occasionally	rarely	never
always	often	I set goals that keep my attitude positive	occasionally	rarely	never

Section Two – Peak Riding Performance

always	often	I ride mentally relaxed	occasionally	rarely	never
always	often	I ride with an optimistic attitude	occasionally	rarely	never
always	often	I act confident in all riding situations	occasionally	rarely	never
always	often	I feel energized when I ride	occasionally	rarely	never
always	often	I sense time slows down when I ride	occasionally	rarely	never
always	often	I feel perfect body awareness	occasionally	rarely	never
always	often	I feel internal calmness when I ride	occasionally	rarely	never
always	often	I feel detached from distractions	occasionally	rarely	never
always	often	I ride in complete control	occasionally	rarely	never
always	often	I ride with clear concentration	occasionally	rarely	never
always	often	I school as if I'm showing	occasionally	rarely	never
always	often	I imagine my ride before showing	occasionally	rarely	never
always	often	I know what causes me anxiety	occasionally	rarely	never
always	often	I use positive brain babble	occasionally	rarely	never
always	often	I ignore "trash-talkers"	occasionally	rarely	never
always	often	I breathe deeply to lessen anxiety	occasionally	rarely	never
always	often	I use a sound as a concentration cue	occasionally	rarely	never
always	often	I use a location as a concentration cue	occasionally	rarely	never
always	often	I use a movement as a concentration cue	occasionally	rarely	never

Section Three – Mental Imagery

always	often	I use all five senses when visualizing	occasionally	rarely	never
always	often	My images are funny	occasionally	rarely	never
always	often	I use imagery before I ride	occasionally	rarely	never
always	often	I use imagery during a ride	occasionally	rarely	never
always	often	I use imagery after I ride	occasionally	rarely	never
always	often	I use imagery to correct problems	occasionally	rarely	never
always	often	I use imagery to learn a new skill	occasionally	rarely	never
always	often	I use imagery to relax	occasionally	rarely	never
always	often	I use imagery to learn from the past	occasionally	rarely	never
always	often	I use imagery to plan future rides	occasionally	rarely	never
always	often	I use videos and photos to improve imagery	occasionally	rarely	never
always	often	I use a movement bridge	occasionally	rarely	never
always	often	I touch the actual object used in my imagery	occasionally	rarely	never
always	often	I visualize I am someone else	occasionally	rarely	never
always	often	I tell my images to others	occasionally	rarely	never
always	often	I relax while I visualize	occasionally	rarely	never
always	often	I use internal imagery	occasionally	rarely	never
always	often	I use external imagery	occasionally	rarely	never

A FINAL THOUGHT

WHILE THE TITLE OF THIS BOOK IS *RIDE RIGHT,* I can't stress enough that there's really no right or wrong way to ride as long as you do so with regard and respect for your body and that of your horse. Teach your mind to translate the language of your horse's body in much the same way that he's learned to translate the language of your body. Listen, *really* listen, to what his body is telling you, and learn to delay the process of judging or blaming him for an apparent imperfection until you're certain that it hasn't been caused by your body, or a simple missed communication between yours and his. Remember that no one cares for your horse more than you, so dedicate yourself to the worthy task of not only improving his competence, but his confidence as well. One of the best ways to accomplish this is by taking the time to improve your own *frame* and *frame of mind.* In the end, your horse's *frame* and *frame of mind* will be the happy recipients of your effort.

RESOURCES

Stable boards, exercise balls, medicine balls, and resistance bands can all be ordered directly from Daniel Stewart's website www.RideRightNow.com. Also, visit his website for information on his mounted and unmounted clinics and workshops.

BIBLIOGRAPHY

American Council on Exercise. "Benedict Harris Formula: Nutrition Basic Concepts and Applications." In *Ace Personal Trainers Manual*. 1991.

Bailey, Covert. *Smart Exercise: Burning Fat, Getting Fit*. New York: Houghton Mifflin Company, 1994.

Golding, Lawrence A., et al. *Y's Way to Physical Fitness: The Complete Guide to Fitness Testing and Instruction*. 3rd ed. Champaign, IL: Human Kinetics Publishing, 1989.

Gould, Daniel. "Goal-Setting for Peak Performance." In *Applied Sport Psychology*. Palo Alto, CA: Mayfield Publishing, 1986.

Hanna, Joyce, Elizabeth Wright, Kay Yoong, and Laura Brainin. "Health and Fitness Assessment." Skylonda Fitness Retreat.

Hill, Cherry. *Becoming an Effective Rider: Develop Your Mind and Body for Balance and Unity*. North Adams, MA: Storey Books, 1991.

Kapit, Wynn, and Lawrence M. Elson. *The Anatomy Coloring Book*. 3rd ed. Glenview, IL: Benjamina Cummings, 2001.

Loehr, James E. *Mental Toughness Training for Sports: Achieving Athletic Excellence*. Lexington, MA: Steven Greene Press, 1982.

Martens, Rainer. *Coaches Guide to Sport Psychology*. Champaign, IL: Human Kinetics Publishing, 1987.

Ravizza, Kenneth. *Relaxation Training for Athletes and Coaches*. Ottawa, CA: Coaching Association of Canada, 1985.

Swift, Sally. *Centered Riding*. North Pomfret, VT: Trafalgar Square Publishing, 1985.

Vealey, Robin S. "Imagery Training for Performance Enhancement." In *Applied Sport Psychology*. Palo Alto, CA: Mayfield Publishing, 1986.

Williams, Jean. "Psychological Characteristics of Peak Performance." In *Applied Sport Psychology*. Palo Alto, CA: Mayfield Publishing, 1986.

INDEX

Page numbers in *italic* indicate illustrations.